CALL SIGNS

How Knowing God's Character Empowers Women to Accomplish His Mission

By Jennifer Wake

Acknowledgments

Thank you to my wonderful husband, who encouraged me to follow my dream of writing and speaking about God. Thank you for working on all the formatting and never letting me give up. I love you more.

Thank you to my wonderful children, who taught me to be a better mom and Christian. I love you very much and am proud of all of you.

Thank you to my sisters, who challenge me to never give up and to always learn. Thank you for being such strong, independent women. I am blessed to be one of the "Miller Girls', I love you both so much.

To my editor Liz Giertz, thank you for putting up with this brand new writer. Your tireless efforts moved me from thinking about publishing to actually doing it. Thank you for encouraging me and never giving up!

To Mary Frances Booth, thank you for believing in me, keeping me grounded, and speaking life into me for years.

To all my PWOC friends near and far, I pray that you will grow closer to God and pursue Him with all your heart!

To my tribe at Planting Roots, thank you for helping me grow closer to God through deep friendships, engaging conferences, and plenty of laughter — especially thanks to Andrea Plotner, who recognized my identity as a writer long before I realized it myself.

INTRODUCTION

Have you ever run from something you knew you should do?

About ten years ago, I knew I was supposed to study the names of God. A friend and I talked about how many times the word "God" appeared in Scripture. That English word appears more often than any other in the Bible. But it is used to cover a wide array of ideas scholars translated from Hebrew, Greek, and Aramaic. I wanted to learn more, but one book I selected had 50 names for God. Another contained a new name for each day of the year. There is even a song that lists each name for God in the Bible. So, I ran.

Until God literally stopped me in my tracks. My husband, Dave, who is an Army chaplain, and I were preparing our home to rent before our move from South Carolina to Texas. I climbed on a stool to fix the peeling popcorn ceiling in our kitchen. During my descent, I missed the last step and landed on my ankle.

Dave drove me to the ER and after one look at my x-rays, the doctor told me I had broken my leg in three places and dislocated my ankle. He sent me home with pain pills and strict instructions to keep my leg immobile and elevated. Now, God had me right where He wanted me. My stillness and desperation created just the training ground He needed to teach me about His names. Every situation and circumstance that presented itself gave Him the opportunity to reveal a new aspect of His character. He showed me how important it is to know His attributes in my time of need, in my time of rest, in my everyday life. As I started to learn about His Call Signs, He planted a seed in my heart which He tended. This seed grew into a mission.

I wanted to learn about God in the New Testament, instead, He drew me to start at the beginning, to learn about His Hebrew names. The Old Testament can be intimidating and it is full of names I can't pronounce. Yet, the Hebrew people announced and demonstrated God's character and attributes through the many names they used to call out to Him in prayer--God's Call Signs.

Prayer is simply a means of communication with God. As believers, we have the privilege of calling on Him by name. And there is a name that provides for every need, solves every problem, wins every battle, and comforts every pain. This realization provided the inspiration for this book.

***
The more we know God,
the more powerful and effective our prayers become.
***

Do you remember the movie *Top Gun*? Tom Cruise's fellow aviators call him "Maverick" and his co-pilot "Goose." These names are military Call Signs. The concept is similar to when children choose nicknames for each other. In the military, you don't get to choose your own call sign, the people who know you best decide on your call sign. It becomes your nickname and communicates different attributes about you.

Military members use Call Signs to designate their position, area of responsibility, and authority. In the heat of battle, it is critical to know who you are calling and why. You wouldn't call a personnel specialist when you need an airstrike or an intelligence analyst when you need a medic. It is important to trust the person you call can meet your needs.

Each military member has a specific mission within the military. The seed God placed in my heart to learn about His names, grew into a mission. My mission was to write about His Call Signs and tell the people around me about Him, to share about His attributes and how they impact our lives, our prayers, and our missions. Jesus gave us the Great Commission in Matthew 28:16-20. He also gives us our own personal mission. Your mission will be different from mine and it will change over time. The more I learned about God the more prepared for my mission I became. With the preparation also came attacks, setbacks, discouragement, and excitement. In every challenge I faced following my injury, God proved He was capable of meeting my every need.

Delving into some of the Call Signs people in the Bible used to call on God, led me to a greater understanding of His attributes and empowered my prayer life. God has many Call Signs, names people called God as they learned about his attributes. We will study one of the names God gave himself, Elohim, as well as others such as Adonai, El Shaddai, and El Roi. Each Call Sign shows an attribute, a part of the character of God. We will discover El Roi, The Lord Sees, in many stories of the Old and New Testaments. From Genesis to Revelation, El Roi sees where His faithful believers are; He is never surprised by what happens. Even in today's uncertain times, with military deployments and civil unrest, El Roi sees each of us and is with us. Just as He loved and watched over the Israelites in Egypt and in the desert, He watches over us and loves us today. Many times our circumstances make us feel alone—deployments, the heartache of miscarriage, loss of family members—but El Shaddai, the All-Sufficient One, is waiting to hold us as we cry out to Him.

This book covers six Call Signs for God that speak to the challenges all women face in every stage of life. But as my original and overwhelming research proves, there are many more names for God in the Bible. This study is designed to help you identify other Call Signs in Scripture, and give you the confidence to pray those attributes back to God. After studying God's Call Signs, you will be empowered to accomplish God's Mission in your life.

God doesn't change; we simply experience different facets of His character. He has so many Call Signs because He has so many attributes. Some attributes are descriptive like Exalted One or God of Sight. Others are revealed by God to people, like the Lord Our Provider, or Healer, or Shepherd or Our peace. God has several Call Signs which He called Himself. Creator, Self-Existent One, All-Sufficient One, and Lord and Master are the Call Signs He used to help people understand who He is. Knowing His character is critical because it gives us the confidence to know when we call out He will answer.

Call Signs is a Bible study to help women grow in their understanding of the attributes of God. The goal is for women to be empowered to pray each name back to God as a form of worship and accomplish His mission wherever He places you. We will study one name each week for ten weeks. You can do the study on your own or in a small group setting. Each Call Sign concludes with a prayer to get you started and some discussion questions to help you see how to apply God's character to your own life.

As a fellow daughter of El Elyon, the Lord Most High, I have prayed that El Shaddai (The All-Sufficient One) would minister to your every need as you discover ways to connect with Elohim (our Creator) more deeply through His Word, worship, and prayer.

Jennifer

Table of Contents

ACKNOWLEDGMENTS	iii
INTRODUCTION	v
1. ELOHIM: CREATOR	1
Prayer to Elohim	13
Questions for Discussion	15
2. EL SHADDAI: THE ALL-SUFFICIENT ONE	19
Prayer to El Shaddai	29
Questions for Discussion	31
3. ADONAI: LORD AND MASTER	35
Prayer to Adonai	47
Questions for Discussion	49
4. EL ELYON: THE LORD MOST HIGH	53
Prayer to El Elyon	61
Questions for Discussion	63
5. EL QANNA: THE LORD IS JEALOUS	67
Prayer to El Qanna	79
Questions for Discussion	81
6. ABBA: FATHER	85
Prayer to Abba	97
Questions for Discussion	99
Charlie Mike: Continue the Mission	103
Sample Call Sign Worksheet	105
Leaders Guide	107
Appendix A – How to Read the Bible for Personal Study	109
Appendix B – How to Memorize Scripture	111
Appendix C – How to Pray	113
Appendix D – What does it mean to be a Christian	115
Endnotes	117

1. ELOHIM: CREATOR

***Elohim entrusts us with His Creation;
we must thank and praise Him.***

One of my favorite things to do is watch storm clouds roll in over the mountains in Colorado or the plains in Kansas. Each storm is unique, the way the wind blows, the clouds move, the lightning streaks across the sky, even how the rain falls to the earth. These storms remind me of Elohim, Our Creator. He created everything from the smallest subatomic particle to the largest hypergiant stars in the universe. Look at leaves around you or snowflakes that fall gently onto your coat, all are different and proclaim God is our Creator.

Sometimes, though, when things are broken, it can be hard to imagine they were divinely created or that they can ever be restored to their former glory.

Miscarriages, broken trust in a marriage, emotional wounds, and so many more hurts cause us to feel broken both inside and out.

After my leg started to heal, I had nightmares about when it was broken. I saw my ankle in its "deformed state" (That's what the EMT called it!). When I was waiting for the ambulance, I did not want to look at my leg for any length of time because I didn't want to remember how it had looked that day. In the ER, the doctors had to cut off the splint the EMT put on to stabilize it. In spite of the pain medicine, the cutting of the tape made me scream in pain. I begged them to let me go home because I couldn't bear the thought of them touching it again. It felt like they were pushing needles through my skin. The swelling had stretched my skin beyond anything I had ever experienced. I thought the pain medicine would take the pain away; it did not help. As gentle as they tried to be, my ankle moved a tiny bit when the nurse removed the splint and caused more screaming. I truly did not think I could handle any more. Due to the dislocation, the doctor had to put the ankle back in alignment, even though the bones were broken. More screaming and more begging them to stop. Finally, they put it in a new cast to keep it in one position to prepare it for surgery.

The staff left me to sit and cry. I sobbed to God to take away this pain. As I waited for Dave to return with the car, I looked at my new cast. My leg was huge! It looked like an elephant's leg but it was now not as deformed as it was at first look. Dave returned and calmed me down with a hug. He looked at me with eyes of love. I said I was deformed, but Dave reminded me he loves me and so does God. God created me with all His love. He loves me perfectly even when I mess up or feel like I am a mess.

The swelling went down and my leg looked less like an elephant and more like my other leg. The doctors told me to keep it elevated all the time to help avoid permanent swelling and discoloration. I tried to obey but sitting all day with my leg elevated was tiring. I behaved myself for about three weeks. Then I started using a scooter to get around instead of elevating it. Of course, I needed to learn more about this Call Sign, because I did not understand how God created me. Elohim had to teach me about how He created us to heal.

Elohim is the first Call Sign for God we find in Scripture. Genesis 1:1 says, "In the beginning God (*Elohim*) created the heavens and the earth." Old Testament writers used it frequently and it means Creator. He created everything, including how we heal. Everything I see, taste, touch, feel, and sense… *everything*.

Elohim is the plural of "might or power."[1] God the Father, God the Son, and God the Holy Spirit created everything. They are the Trinity, Three In One. They alone have the power and might to create something out of nothing. Many of the other Call Signs are plural, too, like Jehovah and Adonai.

The day my stitches came out and the cast went on, I began to worry and fret. I wanted to be completely healed. Instead of confirming my wishes, the doctor warned me I might need the screws taken out and go through this again. I worried about having another surgery because Dave had orders for us to move to Texas. *Will I find a doctor who can help me? Will I walk again?* I questioned God. I did not trust Him and doubted His ability to create another doctor to help me.

As I was praying one morning, Psalm 139 came to mind:

> *"For you formed my inward parts;*
> *you knitted me together in my mother's womb.*
> *I praise you, for I am fearfully and wonderfully made;*
> *Wonderful are your works; my soul knows it very well."*
> Psalm 139:13-14

Years before my accident, God provided Psalm 139:13-14 to help me get through three miscarriages between my oldest and youngest children. Sometimes these words bring me peace and comfort and other times they challenge my faith and remind me of painful times.

As a girl, I dreamed of being a mother. Rachel is my firstborn. Because we got pregnant so quickly after stopping birth control, I wasn't surprised that I got pregnant again when we started trying. Dave was in seminary and I was teaching full time, so when we were offered a "free" ultrasound, we agreed. I remember all these people coming in to "watch and learn" about this new ultrasound system. We didn't care who came in; we were just excited to see our next child. As they moved the machine around, no one spoke. One terse look from the lead technician sent everyone else scrambling out the door without saying a word. DEAD SILENCE. We looked at the screen. On the screen was our perfect baby—arms straight out and legs straight down reminding me of Jesus on the cross. Our baby was perfect, except he did not have a heartbeat. Matter-of-factly she told us, "the fetus had died." Time stopped. I wanted to scream that the baby was still there. Instead, I numbly took the appointment card to come back for the necessary procedure.

We named him Timothy. Then we lost, Grace. And after her, Christopher. They are the children I did not carry to term, and they are up in heaven perfectly and wonderfully made, just not for me to hold right now. They all died before they could live outside my womb. The doctors told me that these "fetuses," my babies, often have too many "genetic mistakes" which don't allow them to form correctly so they can't survive. I don't know if that is true. I believe Elohim created them and that when I meet them, they will be just as He wants them to be. I do not believe He makes mistakes. I wonder if He uses unborn children to teach us things we need to learn, or maybe He takes them to avoid some kind of pain or hard life. I don't know. Whatever the reason He created my three babies who did not stay with me, I know now He has a plan and I need to wait until Jesus comes again to understand it.

I wondered why these verses came to mind as I went to get my stitches removed. Yes, you can see it—stitches in the verse and stitches in me. Elohim used these verses to again reassure me that He is my Creator. God created my leg and ankle and He could change my view of my leg into His view of my leg. Now I am not a supermodel, and no one will ensure my legs for millions of dollars, but my Elohim created them wonderfully. He helped me look at my leg as something that had sustained injury but would heal, instead of being worried it would stay broken forever. Elohim also created a new kind of wonder in my heart about my leg. I often worried if I would walk again or if my leg would just break when I stood on it. My Creator wove me together in my mother's womb and knit my leg together again using four screws, a surgeon, and time. As I sat and recovered, my leg began to heal and knit back together, just as Elohim created it to do.

After my leg was put into a cast and I was allowed to move around a little bit, I started to see God's creation in different ways. Have you ever watched leaves (or in South Carolina— pine straw) fall from a tree? I had the joy of sitting and watching. I watched the branches sway and I tried to figure out which piece of straw would fall next. I never got it right. God created trees to lose their leaves to get ready for winter and the time to rest after the busy part of the year. Elohim created them to store up energy so they would be ready after winter to spring forth.

***

***Elohim entrusts us with His Creation;
we must thank and praise Him.***

***

Just like trees and plants, we go through cycles. God created the heavens and the earth and all things, and then He rested on the seventh day. If God rested and commanded us to rest, it must be important. Trees and animals know the cycle of work and rest. In the Spring, we think of new life, new babies all around us. Giving birth (whether to babies or new leaves) takes energy and strength. Then through the summer, everything grows and gets bigger and stronger, acquiring more energy. By autumn, things start producing fruit and then harvest time finds them storing up supplies for winter. When winter comes, plants rest, animals spend more time sleeping, and days are shorter and darker. This cycle was brought to mind while I was resting.

> *"Yours is the day, yours also the night;*
> *you have established the heavenly lights and the sun.*
> *You have fixed all the boundaries of the earth;*
> *you have made summer and winter."*
> Psalm 74:16-17

Then God took me to Genesis. I once thought I knew all about this book, but God continues to amaze me with new truths in these storied pages. Elohim gave us His creation to care for, nurture, and use. He connects His creation to us and to His rest.

> *Then God said, "Let us make man in our image, after our likeness. And let them have dominion over the fish of the sea and over the birds of the heavens and over the livestock and over all the earth and over every creeping thing that creeps on the earth." So God created man in his own image, in the image of God he created him; male and female he created them. And God blessed them. And God said to them, "Be fruitful and multiply and fill the earth and subdue it, and have dominion over the fish of the sea and over the birds of the heavens and over every living thing that moves on the earth." And God said, "Behold, I have given you every plant yielding seed that is on the face of all the earth, and every tree with seed in its fruit. You shall have them for food. And to every beast of the earth and to every bird of the heavens and to everything that creeps on the earth, everything that has the breath of life, I have given every green plant for food." And it was so.*
> Genesis 1:26-30

Elohim created everything and then gave them to humans to control, care for, and use for food. He provided for their every need. This was the sixth day of creation. Elohim created and then blessed mankind with provisions for life. He gave them their mission to care for the plants and animals.

I am a servant. One of my main love languages is Acts of Service. Gary Chapman defines Acts of Service in his book *The Five Love Languages: How to Express Heartfelt Commitment to Your Mate* as: "Doing things you know your spouse would like you to do. You seek to please her by serving her, to express your love for her by doing things for her."² I show my family and friends that I love them by serving. I don't mind setting up for or cleaning up after an event. Give me a task that would benefit a group, and I will do it.

Before my accident, I served on the board of my local women's ministry as the 1st Vice President in charge of Spiritual Life. The board selected me in May and I began by writing and organizing the summer Bible study. Going into the chapel early and setting up everything was an act of service for me. Writing the study and a short play to kick it off was a great deal more challenging than I ever thought it would be. I knew God wanted me to do it and He gave me the words, but I worried and fretted over how it would be received. I craved "Words of Affirmation" since this was totally new to me. But as I let God lead my writing, He created in me the desire to study and write more.

At the end of the summer study, I continued my work as 1st VP, which included choosing Bible Studies, organizing devotions, and praying. I continued to serve, but my emotional "love tank" was empty. The different love languages fill this tank. I show love by Acts of Service, but I get love into my tank primarily by Quality Time. I love spending time with Dave and our kids. Sitting and talking or watching TV will give me enough gas to keep going. At the end of the summer, we found out Dave had orders to report to Texas in December. I decided, without asking Dave or God, that the kids and I would stay in South Carolina until May so Rachel could finish her sophomore year. Neither Dave nor God liked this plan, but I thought I knew best. I made plans for that separation and most conversations Dave and I had centered on how to live separately. Instead of filling my tank with quality time, I realized I would be alone for seven months and my love tank began to leak.

I felt like I had nothing left to give. And then I broke my ankle which completely emptied my tank. But then my good friend Kendra reminded me of the yearly cycle of seasons. She reminded me that we all seem to love spring and summer and some even love fall. But most of us just want winter to end (after Christmas is over). But God wants us to rest during our winter so we can be ready for the next spring, summer, and fall. As I rested in my inability to do anything let alone serve, God showed me his name Elohim. We are God's creation. God the Father, God the Son, and God the Holy Spirit were all involved in the creation of the world. After they created everything, they rested. I realized I need rest, too.

My Elohim created the world with cycles of starting a ministry, growing a ministry, and harvesting but also resting from ministry.

> *For everything there is a season, and a time for every matter under heaven:*
> *a time to be born and a time to die;*
> *a time to plant and a time to pluck up what is planted;*
> *a time to kill and a time to heal;*
> *a time to break down, and a time to build up;*
> *a time to weep, and a time to laugh;*
> *a time to mourn, and a time to dance;*
> *a time to cast away stones, and a time to gather stones together;*
> *a time to embrace, and a time to refrain from embracing;*
> *a time to seek, and a time to lose;*
> *a time to keep, and a time to cast away;*
> *a time to tear, and a time to sew;*
> *a time to keep silent, and a time to speak;*
> *a time to love, and a time to hate;*
> *a time for war, and a time for peace.*
> Ecclesiastes 3:1-8

Just as Elohim rested for a time, I needed to rest from serving for a time. My mission changed from serving others to resting and learning to accept help from others. I rested from housework, from serving on the Protestant Women Of the Chapel (PWOC) board, from helping at Chapel, from so many acts of service. I rested and people were still blessed. The Protestant Women Of the Chapel board stepped up and filled in everywhere. The chapel family filled in.

My children helped with the housework. In fact, my wonderful fifteen-year-old daughter Rachel came up one day with a basket of laundry and said, "I do not want to do everyone's laundry. This is too much work. It is hard. I come home and put in a load and dry it and it never ends. I didn't know laundry was so much work. You *actually* do a lot of work around the house." My heart leapt for joy; she was learning. After we moved she began to do her own laundry and now does it without help. She became more independent during my season of resting.

Even in my season of forced rest, God was at work, and as I called on Him as Creator of all, He revealed how. He bore fruit in my children, blessed me with strong friendships, filled my love tank, and even created new desires in my heart.

***

Elohim, God our Creator,
created each season of our lives with a mission.
***

Elohim also created in me a desire to write again. After trying my hand at writing a five-week Bible study and a short play to introduce it, I assumed I was done writing. I enjoy teaching and learning, but writing was not something I felt called to do. Since my resting time, I began writing more and more. I like to write and read emails but most of all, I love to write what God burdens my heart with. That is how this book got started. Elohim and the other Call Signs of God enthrall me. My God calls Himself so many things and discovering the origins of those names and their significance in my life fascinates me.

***

Elohim created us to worship Him and to thank Him,
so we need to look for His blessings daily.
***

Sometimes I needed to look for them hourly since I would forget and start to wallow in self-pity. As I wrote the lessons I was learning, God impressed on my heart the song "Count Your Blessings" by Johnson Oatman, Jr. The chorus is my favorite part. "Count your blessings, name them one by one." The song continues to remind you that no matter what happens you can look around and see what God has done. Whenever I start to throw myself a pity party, Elohim brings this song to mind to encourage me to see that my life is full of blessings.

***

As we intentionally seek God's blessings in our lives,
we will discover how purposefully He orchestrates every detail.

***

We need to remember that Elohim created differences for a reason. Each of my kids has different hair (one blond and wavy, one reddish-brown with tight curls, one brown, thick, and straight). I have two blue-eyed girls and a brown-eyed boy. None of them are green-eyed like me or hazel like Dave. Yet looking at their faces you can see both my family and Dave's likenesses. How amazing Elohim created them with parts of so many people. How sobering that He entrusted them to my care.

He echoes similar creative concepts in nature. I love walking around upstate NY in the fall, looking at the amazing leaves. My mother planted three saplings many years ago, which came from the same tree at her mom's house. In the summer, these red maples are so beautiful, and they all look the same. However, in the fall, one is bright red, the second is blazing orange, and the third is deep red. If you picked up one leaf from each tree you would not know they came from the seeds of the same tree many years ago. Elohim created each tree and allowed the tree to show off different colors in the fall even though they all came from the same original tree. When I see these beautiful trees, I thank God His creativity is so much greater than mine.

A friend invited my kids over after her dog had puppies. The puppies were about three weeks old and full of life. They all came from the same parents, but boy, they were so different. The mother was a yellow lab, the father a chocolate lab. In the litter, there was one chocolate, and the rest were yellow. But the personalities were already emerging—bossy, quiet, playful. Each puppy had already shown some of his or her characteristics. My friend gave the puppies their Call Signs because of their personalities. Bossy Pants, Sweetheart, and Snuggles. My kids loved playing with the puppies, except for the chewing. Every one of those puppies loved to chew. Elohim made some things different and some things the same.

***

*Elohim has the power, autonomy,
and sovereignty to create as He pleases.*

***

As I sat during my time of healing, I thought about my bones a great deal. God created each bone, each muscle, every part of me with a purpose. Some things like wisdom teeth and tonsils I can live without. Other parts like lungs, liver, heart, I cannot. Yet damaged lungs, liver, or heart, can heal and can be repaired. My very broken leg could be repaired. Skilled surgeons repaired my leg, but God created it. We can't grow replacement legs. Science fiction movies or stories may talk of being able to replace arms or legs with limbs grown for that purpose, but I doubt we will ever be able to do that.

***
God is the Creator, not man.
***

I constantly remind myself that I am not Elohim. That one statement reminds me that, although I gave birth, God created my children. He created them very differently. Andrew is 100% boy; which means he is into bombs, guns, and destroying things. He is also sweet, loving, smart yet unmotivated most of the time. Dena is my mini-me so she is driven, intelligent, diligent, and also loves sports and competitions. Rachel is my fashion girl, who is like her brother, smart, sweet, and usually unmotivated. Their eyes and hair are different from each other, yet they come from one set of parents. God created them each with their own unique attributes. Elohim loves variety.

Elohim, the Creator, was the first Call Sign. Seeing and pondering all the variety God created in the world and feeling the weight of the responsibility to care for it He has entrusted to me, empowers me to praise and thank Elohim. His creativity and unending diversity reminds me of His love for every single part of me and my life. This Call Sign draws me to praise Him every day. Let's spend some time counting our blessings before we move to learn more about God through His Call Sign, El Shaddai.

Prayer to Elohim

Elohim our Creator,
You give us so much.
You created the air we breathe.
The water and food we need to live.

Bluebirds, red Cardinals, Nuthatches, Mockingbirds, all sing so differently to wake us up.
Bright sunshine, deep dark nights are all from you.
Green grass, shade trees, breezes to cool us in the summer heat.
Ice, snow, crisp mornings, clear nights to help us enjoy wintertime.
Rainy, foggy, and cloudy days are all from You.
Thank You, Elohim, Our Creator.

Children, young and not so young all laugh contagiously to help us enjoy the day.
Big dogs, small cats, animals of all sizes come from you.
Laughter with dear friends, even tears to help us heal.
Smiles, frowns, faces full of wonder remind us of Your love.
Quiet, loud, reflective mornings are all from You.
Thank You, Elohim, Our Creator.

There are times of plenty, and times of want.
Overstuffed mouths and bellies full of wonderful food come from Elohim.
Hungry people looking for food, love, and acceptance remind us to share You.
People who are lost need Your touch today.
Feelings of plenty, want, satisfaction, are all from You.
Thank You, Elohim, Our Creator.

Families who are missing their loved ones need Your touch.
Military members, who may be far from home, are never far from Elohim.
Children who are waiting for their mom or dad to return look to You for peace.
Elohim our Creator has made all of us.
He has created the ultimate sacrifice for us.
The sacrifice of love, Jesus.
Thank You, Elohim, Our Creator.
Amen.

Questions for Discussion

These questions can be used for personal study or for group discussion.

1. List some different ways Elohim created people or things in your current situations. Take time to thank Him.

2. Can you count all your blessings? Try It. This may take a very long time. Try to spend a few minutes each day this week counting your blessings.

3. Have you told Elohim that you like how He created you? Take time right now to thank Him, be specific.

4. In what areas of your life are you dissatisfied? How can remembering that Elohim doesn't make mistakes help in those areas?

5. When you see people with disabilities, what do you think about it? Do you think our Creator ever makes mistakes? Take a look at John 9. This is the story of the healing of the blind man.

6. Elohim is a name you can get lost in. It has so many parts. Elohim is both an adjective and a verb. Elohim is very active. Look the following verses up and match adjectives and verbs describing Elohim (LORD in most translations) to the verse.

Joshua 24:19	Living God
2 Samuel 7:22	The Lord of Hosts
Psalm 99:8	Faithful
Deuteronomy 7:9	Merciful and gracious
Deuteronomy 10:17	The great, the almighty one
Jeremiah 32:18	None like you.
Exodus 34: 6	Forgiving
2 Kings 19:16	Jealous

7. How will your increased understanding of God as Elohim, empower your prayer life? Write out a prayer to Elohim claiming the promises and character of God indicated by this Call Sign. Step outside, take a few minutes to contemplate God's purpose for every bit of creation you can see. Now praise Elohim for His creativity. Thank Him for all the different people around you. Praise Him for all the ways He created you uniquely.

Notes:

2. *EL SHADDAI: THE ALL-SUFFICIENT ONE*

El Shaddai desires us to breathe in His power and strength through prayer so we will learn to trust Him in all areas of our lives.

When I started this journey to study the Call Signs of God little did I know where it would take me. El Shaddai is "The All-sufficient One." This name seemed too easy. Of course, God is the All-Sufficient One. He can do anything, He is all-knowing, all-powerful, eternal. Yet that just scratches the surface of El Shaddai.

God's Call Sign, El Shaddai comes from the Hebrew word SHAD meaning "breasted." That made me stop and ponder for quite a while. My picture of God makes him a male. SHAD is used to mean giving milk from a breast. I call out to my Father, not to a mother. Digging further, this Call Sign means giving or sustaining life. Breast milk is life-giving nourishment for babies.

As I began to ponder this, I remember breastfeeding both Rachel and Dena. Women told me nursing was a wonderful bonding experience. It even helped some mothers lose weight, which of course, I wanted to do. Excited to bond with Rachel, we began our journey of nursing. Although we nursed every two hours, Rachel did not make back her birth weight for more than six weeks. I left every weekly appointment feeling like a failure. I worked with several lactation specialists who kept telling me to try again. Rachel and I struggled until I started her on formula at four months. When I told the lactation specialist what I was doing she said, "Well your daughter will not do well in the future. You have failed her." I wanted to crawl into a hole; instead, I started crying and worrying.

Five years after I tried and failed at nursing with Rachel, I heard the same dreaded words about our younger daughter, "Your baby, Dena, is not making back her birth weight." Tears started flowing, then full-on sobbing. This time, our pediatrician was a family friend who let me sob and assured me Dena would not end up scarred for life if I switched away from nursing. When I had calmed down enough to hear it, he shared his philosophy about feeding a newborn. He told me it had two main goals—one was nourishment and the other was bonding. He realized the stress of nursing was causing me not to bond with Dena. His words sunk deep into my heart, allowing me the freedom to decide to stop breastfeeding. Today, both Dena and Rachel are beautiful, intelligent, young women.

This Call sign, El Shaddai, reminded me of the pediatrician's words. El Shaddai wants to bond with us by nourishing our souls. He wants us to enjoy a special time with Him. His Word is our milk and meat to help us grow.

***

Prayer is our time to share our hearts with El Shaddai and connect with Him.
***

He gives us His Holy Spirit to give us life. When you say El Shaddai, do you feel yourself exhaling at the end? As you breathe out, God will send His Spirit to fill you. I picture God waiting for us to stop, to say El Shaddai, and then He comes and fills us. We must breathe in El Shaddai.

My absolute favorite smell is mulled apple cider. It brings back smells of home, sitting by a fire, watching football games. My mom made it after a morning of raking the carpet of leaves that covered our lawn. I remember taking deep breaths of apples, cinnamon, cloves, and many other spices. El Shaddai wants us to breathe in His power, His strength, His peace. He wants us to desire sweet time with Him and He wants to sustain us. Whenever I smell mulled cider, I remember warmth and family.

***

> *Whenever I say El Shaddai,*
> *I think of power, strength, peace, and mercy.*

***

After I was cleared to do physical therapy on my ankle, I was told I had lost all muscle tone in both legs. I don't think the physical therapists realized how little I had to start with, but now I had none. So I did physical therapy to strengthen my muscles. When I was done with my official physical therapy, the therapist recommended I start doing yoga. Now, yoga to me is a very "new age" practice and not something I thought about doing. Plus picturing me trying to bend into some of the poses made me laugh. Because I wanted to continue strengthening my muscles, I decided I would try it. As I tried to do the poses for yoga I realized I no longer bend like I did when I was in college. Yes, that was 30 years ago but in my mind, I have not aged much.

I am certain it was no mere coincidence that I started yoga while I was studying this Call Sign. The first pose is the pose for breathing. Yes, yoga has a pose for breathing. It starts with clearing your mind. What came to my mind was El Shaddai. As I breathed in, I focused on God filling me with His Spirit. I pictured Him smiling at my poses and lack of grace. This focus on God helped me bend in ways I never thought possible.

I enjoy doing yoga as I focus on El Shaddai, but as Christians, we need to be aware of some potential dangers associated with the practice. In one class I attended, the yoga instructor talked about breathing in spirits who will change you and cleanse you. These spirits may not be from God, so I focused on El Shaddai.

We use verbs like bend, shape, and knead in yoga, cooking, and art. These are verbs I know God likes. He uses them when it comes to my spirit, my service, and my mission. He wants to shape me like clay. But to shape clay, you have to knead it a bit to make it malleable. My will and my personality are hard sometimes, ok most of the time. Even though I know He is my All-Sufficient One, I still stubbornly try to do things in my own strength. As I focus on the Call Sign, El Shaddai, I let Him knead my spirit, bend my will, and shape my heart.

Over the years, El Shaddai has provided some other opportunities to knead, bend, and shape me. When we first joined the Army, we were stationed in Colorado. I was invited to Protestant Women of the Chapel (PWOC) by a couple of ladies who came to meet me as soon as we moved in. They picked me up and took me to the chapel on the first day so I would not have to walk in alone. It was a great introduction to Army life, as well as PWOC.

At PWOC, I grew in my faith and met many ladies who became lifelong friends. A few months later, one of the more mature ladies asked us to raise our hands if we attended chapel on the post. Since my husband was a chaplain, we attended chapel. Little did I understand what she was actually asking. She was the head of the committee to choose who would serve on the board the following year. The committee asked me to pray over becoming president. After allowing God to knead my heart, I hesitantly agreed to serve as president for the next year. What an amazing year! God used this service to teach me not just about the organization but about leadership.

***

Every day El Shaddai filled me with His Spirit and showed me He was enough.
***

The two ladies who were my Vice-Presidents were my anchors; Lynda and Jenny taught me so much. They did most of the work and I prayed. El Shaddai was growing leadership within my heart. Being a leader does not mean doing everything, instead, it often means delegating to others after sharing God's vision. I wanted to step in and take over but El Shaddai stopped me. His plan was perfect, Lynda and Jenny followed Him closely. Most of that year as president, I spent on my knees letting El Shaddai knead me, bend me, and shape me.

After that year, the Lord burdened my heart that I was not to serve in that position again. People frequently tell me that my role as a chaplain's wife and the personality God created in me, make me seem like the perfect candidate. But He placed this prohibition against serving as president deep into my heart, so I now serve in different roles within Protestant Women of the Chapel and other

women's ministries.

After five years in Germany, El Shaddai moved us to Fort Irwin, California. Just before we left Fort Irwin, a friend on the regional board asked me to serve on the Protestant Women of the Chapel Western Region's Selection committee. This team of ladies selected the Protestant Women Of The Chapel Western Region's board. I did not have any experience with regional-level boards. As I accepted this job, I started to feel God pushing on my heart. As the outgoing regional board prayed over us, one lady prayed God would knead me. They spoke of kneading bread dough to make it rise and become larger than it was at the beginning. As I look back on that special time, I see El Shaddai is the air mixing with me to "raise my ministry".

***

God kneaded me and I started to bend, expand, and grow.

***

El Shaddai used the fall of 2009 with a friend, Kendra, to breathe a passion for writing into my heart. Kendra and I met for a brief time at Fort Irwin in 2006. We reconnected at a conference where we spent a couple of hours discussing how God wants to lift up the next generation of teachers. She and I skipped a workshop to sit and talk. It was a life-changing talk, but I did not realize it at the time. El Shaddai, my All-Sufficient One, had more kneading to do.

El Shaddai burdened my heart about His Call Signs. During my healing in the fall of 2010, El Shaddai, my All-Sufficient One, gave me an abundance of topics…His Call Signs. I had to breathe in His Spirit to calm my worry about everything I was going through. I had to learn that His peace would get me through any trials in my path. He took me to Moses to teach me.
In Exodus 4:1-17, Moses learned about Jehovah. Moses met Jehovah at the burning bush and learned about I Am who I Am. (Exodus 3:14) God taught Moses how to describe Jehovah to everyone who questioned him.

***
El Shaddai desires us to breathe in His power and strength through prayer.
***

Yet Moses did not trust God to talk through Him. Although He was angry with Moses, El Shaddai decided to allow Aaron, a cousin of Moses, to speak. In Exodus 4:15b, God said, "I will be with your mouth and with his mouth and will teach you both what to do." I pray as I breathe in El Shaddai, He teaches me what to do and say. As my All-Sufficient One, He teaches me what He wants me to teach to others. If I do not spend time with my El Shaddai I miss out on His wisdom which leads to many mistakes.

Just as El Shaddai had to knead Moses into the leader He wanted Moses to be, He wants to knead us into the people He wants us to be to accomplish the missions He assigns to us. When I first heard the word "knead" I thought it was "need." At first, I wanted God to "need" me. He loves me but I thought He needed me. Once I figured out it was "knead", my whole focus changed. Instead of needing Him to "need" me, I want Him to knead me. Change me, grow me, and make me more like Him, my All-Sufficient One, my El Shaddai.

Kneading is not easy. Look at the mission God gave Moses; he had to leave his home and go to Egypt to stand up to the Pharaoh. When bread dough is being kneaded, the person kneading uses a great deal of strength to work the air into the bread so that the yeast can rise and grow throughout the bread. Sometimes when God kneads me, it is painful. Growth is often painful because we are stretched in ways that are not pleasant but allow, sometimes even force, us to rely on our El Shaddai. As He kneads us, if we become like yeast, we take in the breath of God and grow in the ways He wants us to. If we resist, we become tough and hard. Yeast bread that is not kneaded well will not rise properly. Instead, it will be hard and tough to eat. Moses could have avoided the burning bush and not gone to Egypt, instead, he chose to change and follow El Shaddai.

As I think about El Shaddai, I think about my homemade cinnamon rolls. Shortcuts don't work. Time, temperature, air, and kneading are the elements that make the rolls great. Time with El Shaddai, breathing in His Spirit, accepting the kneading, and being warm (the perfect temperature), are all things that come to mind. When I am lukewarm in my walk with the Lord, I am not surrendering my heart to El Shaddai.

> *"I know your works: you are neither cold nor hot. Would that you were either cold or hot! So, because you are lukewarm, and neither hot nor cold, I will spit you out of my mouth."*
> Revelation 3:15-16

Yeast needs warm (not lukewarm) water to grow. He wants me to grow in Him and be excited about growing closer to Him. He will be beside me as I grow and because He is the All-Sufficient One, I can never outgrow Him.

***

El Shaddai wants me to be on fire for Him,
to be on a mission for Him.

***

Moses had to learn how to stand up to adversity in God's way. When Moses was young he killed an Egyptian man who was beating an Israelite man. Because of this, Moses fled Egypt and lived in Midian for forty years. Then God appeared to him in the burning bush with a task Moses felt ill-equipped to tackle. God wanted Moses to trust Him and rely on His power, not Moses' temper. God told

Moses to confront the pharaoh about keeping the people as slaves. Moses had to bring plagues down on Egypt because the pharaoh refused to let the Israelites leave. I am sure God did not want all those plagues, but sometimes people have hard heads and hearts. El Shaddai grew and stretched Moses into the leader the people needed. He wants to grow and stretch each of us. Spending time with El Shaddai will allow you to grow and stretch to become who God wants you to be.

***

El Shaddai desires us to breathe in His power and strength through time spent learning about Him by reading and meditating on the Bible.

***

El Shaddai is our All-Sufficient one. This reminds me that I need to spend time in His Word, not in books written by other people. I used to rely on books to give me a devotion to study. Now, I use the Bible more. El Shaddai wants us to turn to Him and not to extra books. Anytime we focus more on the writings of a person than the words in the Bible, we are in error. Moses spent time with El Shaddai. God used the days Moses spent with El Shaddai to equip him to lead the people.

Before Jesus' death and resurrection, Peter and all the Apostles spent time with Jesus face to face. They heard His stories and lived life with Him. After the resurrection, the Apostles relied on El Shaddai for the strength and the words to share God's saving grace with the world. In the book of Acts, the Apostles were given the ability to speak different languages so they could go out and share the gospel.

Suddenly being able to speak a new language would have scared me. Not Peter, he boldly stood up and preached and 3,000 souls were added to the fellowship (Acts 2:41). Their All-Sufficient One, El Shaddai, strengthened each of the Apostles and disciples.

***

When we are faced with challenges, El Shaddai strengthens us and grows us.

***

Looking back at my husband's deployments I realized El Shaddai was truly growing and strengthening me. My husband's first deployment started when Rachel was four years old and Dena was two weeks old. My survival was truly a gift from God. Each day was hard but the weeks and months flew by. I remember nights after they were asleep, sitting up and crying out to God for forgiveness. I knew I had failed, yet again, as a mom. Now, neither girl remembers those days. That goes for all my husband's deployments. I always thought I failed as a mom but God has protected my kids through all my mistakes. We had rough days and good days. El Shaddai provided strength and hope through it all. El Shaddai never left me, He grew me as a mom and a believer.

In many ways, El Shaddai is my favorite Call Sign for God. It reminds me that He is everywhere and in every circumstance. He is everything I will ever need. Being an Army spouse means moving. Our moves happen usually every two years, sometimes more often, sometimes less. Throughout our moves, I have learned to be content in whatever housing situation God gives us. My daughter wants us to move to a "bigger" house, but I am content in the house that God has given us. It may not be the newest or biggest but it is sufficient for our needs. God knows that this house is where we need to live. If only I could convince my children.

Sometimes when I feel overwhelmed with "busyness" (not business) I will remember El Shaddai is my All-sufficient One and I can lean on Him to get me through the activities. I am naturally a teacher and leader. I don't like chaos in a group, so if there is a void of leadership I will step in. This makes me appear to be an extrovert. I am not. I am, by nature, an introvert. I like my alone time. Sometimes I crave friends, but during busy weeks I crave alone time. During my introvert time, I lean on El Shaddai to renew me and prepare me for other activities.

El Shaddai desires us to breathe in His power and strength through prayer, time in His Word, and faith in order to learn to trust Him in all areas of our lives. Trusting El Shaddai's plan for our lives means trusting Him in the small things as well as the huge life-changing things. Since El Shaddai is in control of everything, He will breathe into us His power and strength when we spend time with Him. Rest in His strength. When I follow Him closely, I find rest. Following

Him reminds me of Adonai, Our Lord and Master; we'll dig into that Call Sign next.

Prayer to El Shaddai

El Shaddai, the all-sufficient One. You are powerful. You are stronger than anything we face. Breathe Your strength into us.

You are stronger than children's temper tantrums.
You are stronger than loneliness.
You are stronger than toxic leaders.
You are stronger than people who rise up against me.

You are stronger than time.
You are stronger than waves in the ocean.
You are stronger than the wind.
You are stronger than the mountains.

You are mighty like an oak.
You are awesome like the sun.
You are more powerful than an ox.
You are omnipotent.

El Shaddai, breathe Your strength into us.
Breathe Your power into us.
Breathe Your peace into us.
El Shaddai, breathe on us.

Amen.

Questions for Discussion

These questions can be used for personal study or for group discussion.

1. How is El Shaddai growing you?

2. Have you seen or felt God kneading you? If so, in what areas of your life? What is your response to His kneading?

3. What does "All-sufficient One" mean?

4. How did El Shaddai knead the people in these stories?

    a. Noah   (Genesis 5:32-9:28)

    b. Esther   (Book of Esther)

    c. Priscilla   (Acts 18:1, 26; Romans 16:3; 1Corinthians 16:19)

5. El Shaddai gives life to all things. How can you apply this to your life?

6. Picture yourself as a lump of clay. What shape would you like God to mold you into?

7. What areas of your life would you like El Shaddai to change?

8. What verses show El Shaddai changing someone?

9. How will knowing God as El Shaddai, empower you to accomplish your mission? Write out a prayer to El Shaddai claiming the promises and character of God indicated by this Call Sign.

Notes:

3. ADONAI: LORD AND MASTER

Adonai, our Lord and Master, reveals and guides us in our missions.

"God is my co-pilot."

In the never-ending parent pick-up line at my daughter's school, I was behind a blue Honda minivan with this bumper sticker. I chuckled as I sat waiting for the line to start moving. I thought it was a cute saying but then as I pondered it, I wondered if it was true. And if it was true, what did that really mean. A little research revealed co-pilots primarily assist the pilot during take-off and landing and take over if the pilot is incapacitated. If this bumper sticker was right, I was the pilot of my own life and God was just there to help out if I needed Him.

As I studied the Call Signs of God, He took me to Adonai. Adonai means Lord and Master. God revealed to me His truth; Adonai is our pilot, co-pilot, and navigator. He is in control of all parts of His plan and should be in control of all parts of my life and mission. He should be the only one we trust to man the control center of our lives. Jeremiah 29:11 says, "'For I know the plans that I have for you,' declares the LORD, 'plans for welfare and not for calamity to give you a future and a hope.'"

***

As we see Him in His rightful place, we learn about Adonai as Master.

***

Adonai means "Lord and Master." It is plural which reminds us of the Trinity. If we call out to Adonai, we learn what the term "Lord and Master" means. As our Adonai, God supplies what we, as His servants, need to do His mission at the time of His planning. We don't get the supplies too early or too late, but at the perfect time.

Part of the Call Sign Adonai is the term Master. In Old Testament times, the Israelites were slaves, servants, and sometimes masters. A slave was a person owned by another and had no choice in the matter. A servant worked for a family and could change where they worked. A master owned slaves and employed servants. There was also a special category—a bondservant or bond-slave. A bondservant by definition is "a person who is devoted to another to the disregard of one's own interests."[1] The Old Testament talks about setting slaves and servants free in the year of Jubilee.

> *"If your brother, a Hebrew man or a Hebrew woman, is sold to you, he shall serve you six years, and in the seventh year you shall let him go free from you. And when you let him go free from you, you shall not let him go empty-handed. You shall furnish him liberally out of your flock, out of your threshing floor and out of your winepress. As the Lord your God has blessed you, you shall give to him. You shall remember that you were a slave in the land of Egypt, and the LORD your God redeemed you; therefore I command you this today. But if he says to you, 'I will not go out from you,' because he loves you and your household, since he is well-off with you, then you shall take an awl and put it through his ear into the*

> *door, and he shall be your slave forever. Also to your female slave, you shall do the same.*
> Deuteronomy 15:12-17

Bondservants choose to serve a master forever without being forced or held captive. They set aside any ideas of freedom or leaving and choose to remain and belong as part of the family. After they made this choice, they were no longer treated like regular servants. They were trusted with greater responsibilities and sometimes even as friends.

Many New Testament authors use this idea of a bondservant (Greek word doulos) to explain their relationship to the Lord. Some translations use bondservant, others servant. The NKJV uses Bondservant in 2 Peter, Romans 1, and Titus 1. It is also used in James 1:1, Jude 1:1, and Revelation 1:1. This is not a term they would have used lightly. By calling themselves bondservants these apostles acknowledged Adonai as their Master. They chose to serve Adonai with their hearts, minds, and bodies. They chose to stay with Him instead of leaving to go into the world. This term implied a huge commitment for anyone associated with the Israelites. There was no change, no going back, no suing for freedom. This was a very final and complete choice to align with Adonai, the ultimate step of love. Deuteronomy 15:16 says the servant chooses to stay because of love for the master and the household.

Along with the choice comes the knowledge that Adonai is your Master. As Master, Adonai will provide shelter, protection, food, and all necessities (sounds like Jehovah-Jireh). One Call Sign will often lead us to other Call Signs. Adonai, as a Master, will tell His bondservants what to do and how to do it.

Adonai, Our Master, gives us the Great Commission and our personal missions. His Great Commission is to share His message of the Gospel of Christ. We are to live our lives so that people around us know we are Christians. Our personal mission could be to become a missionary to an international location or it could be to witness to your neighbors. I have led mission trips to Jamaica and Kenya, but my family's mission field is military families. I love leading vacation Bible schools, or AWANA programs. I also enjoy teaching women and teens. God has changed my mission several times and I am sure He will change it several more times. He is my Master and I serve where He wants me to serve.

But Adonai means more than Master, it also means Lord. And as our Lord, He expects and deserves our reverence.

***
Let's look at what the term "Lord" means.
***

I spent three years in elementary school in England. England has such a rich heritage of monarchies and very person who visits or lives there learns about the monarchy. As a girl growing up there, I dreamed of becoming a princess by marrying a prince. I even learned that as an American not of royal birth, the only way for me to become a princess was to marry a prince. As I researched the royal family (we called them "the royals"), I learned a great deal about protocol. Whenever you see "a royal" walking with people, look closely at the people around them. When the Queen of England walks, no one walks right in front of her. They are almost always one step behind her; she leads the way. If she decides to turn, everyone will follow where she has decided to go. If she stops, everyone has time to stop and not run into her. By being one step behind her, she can still talk to the people softly so everyone else does not hear. I often wondered about what she said when the people she was with would smile. The Queen does not worry about the things around her because she trusts her bodyguards. She knows her path, her plans, and her people.

Adonai is our King. As such, we ought to learn to walk one step behind Him. Not beside Him, assuming we are His equals. Not too far behind Him where we might lose track of Him. Not in front of Him trying to lead. No, instead we should work daily to walk one step behind where we can share quiet, private conversations, see His path, and notice when He stops to allow us to rest. His presence protects us from things He does not allow, but it doesn't mean He protects us from everything. Sometimes, He allows things we would rather not endure, like trials, to happen to us according to His plans and His timing.

By studying Adonai, we learn that He deserves our respect. Being a person of royal birth comes with some innate protocol. Some people respect royalty, others scorn it. Still, others do not care at all about it. We can neither scorn Him nor be indifferent to His proper place in our lives. Because Adonai means our Lord and Master, we need to show Him respect and reverence. Calling Him Lord means following His plan, even when I want to argue with Him. It is easy to believe I know better when I forget He is Adonai, my Lord and Master.

***
Adonai, our Lord and Master, is in His Throne Room.
***

Adonai is seated on His throne. Romans 8:34 says, "Who is to condemn? Christ Jesus is the one who died—more than that, who was raised—who is at the right hand of God, who indeed is interceding for us." Jesus is seated at His right hand. Because of His sacrifice on the cross, we can enter Adonai's throne room through prayer. Praying gives us access to the throne room and our prayers are part of the smoke from incense (Revelation 8:4). We are to pray without ceasing (1 Thessalonians 5:17).

As I pray, I must remember that as my Lord, I need to fear and reverence Him. The fear and reverence of God is a misunderstood concept. People do not understand what it means to fear God. Proverbs 9:10 states, "The fear of God is the beginning of wisdom, and the knowledge of the Holy One is insight." Psalm 111:10 says, "The fear of the LORD is the beginning of wisdom; all those who practice it have a good understanding. His praise endures forever!" We must look at God in awe.

> *"And now, Israel, what does the Lord your God require of you, but to fear the Lord your God, to walk in all his ways, to love him, to serve the Lord your God with all your heart and with all your soul.*
> *You shall fear the Lord your God. You shall serve him and hold fast to him and by his name you shall swear. He is your praise. He is your God, who has done for you these great and terrifying things your eyes have seen."*
> Deuteronomy 10:12, 20-21

Fearing God means showing proper reverence. He is perfect, all-powerful, all-knowing. He is perfect so He cannot have imperfection near Him. Because He is perfect, He can destroy our world at any time. Yet because of His great love for us, He chooses not to destroy us. Fearing God is acknowledging that He can and should destroy us for our sins, but He shows us mercy and grace instead. He withholds judgment. Many churches teach only about His love but fail to explain how we should fear Him and His righteous wrath. Other churches teach people to fear hell more than they fear God.

***

*The more we learn about the true character of God,
the more we know He is worthy of awe, of reverence, and of fear.*

***

God wants us to understand how much He hates sin and to fear His judgment. He must judge, because He is holy. There is no sin in his presence. He is love, but because He is perfectly good He cannot have sin near Him. He wants us to be with Him forever, but our sins break that fellowship. Only by receiving Jesus Christ as our Lord and Savior will we be cleansed from our sins. Jesus covers our sins with his blood restoring our fellowship with Adonai.

The Lordship of God means total possession of me and my total submission to Him as Lord and Master. He wants me to choose to be His bondservant and submit to Him. He wants us to serve Him with all our hearts, all our minds, and all our souls. Saying He is your Lord and Master, but then not living as He wants you to live proclaims that you do not know Adonai. If you know Adonai you will want to serve Him and follow His Scriptures.

This is what Jesus talked about in Luke.

> *And a ruler asked him, "Good Teacher, what must I do to inherit eternal life?" And Jesus said to him, "Why do you call me good? No one is good except God alone. You know the commandments: 'Do not commit adultery, Do not murder, Do not steal, Do not bear false witness, Honor your father and mother.'" And he said, "All these things I have kept from my youth." When Jesus heard this, he said to him, "One thing you still lack. Sell all that you have and distribute to the poor, and you will have treasure in heaven; and come, follow me." But when he heard these things, he became very sad, for he was extremely rich. Jesus, seeing that he had become sad, said, "How difficult it is for those who have wealth to enter the kingdom of God! For it is easier for a camel to go through the eye of a needle than for a rich person to enter the kingdom of God." Those who heard it said, "Then who can be saved?" But he said, "What is impossible with man is possible with God."*
> Luke 18:18-27

This ruler had followed the rules but had never listened to Adonai. He wanted to keep his money as security because he did not trust God to provide. He wanted to keep control of his financial security instead of allowing Adonai to control every part of his life.

Money is not inherently bad. 1 Timothy 6:10 says, "For the love of money is a root of all kinds of evils. It is through this craving that some have wandered away from the faith and pierced themselves with many pangs." Adonai wants us to look at Him, not at our bank accounts. He promises to provide for us. When we worry about money it becomes an idol in our lives. We have to focus on Him and serve Him. He wants to be Lord and Master of all parts of our lives.

***

> ***Part of being a bondservant is learning
> to serve Adonai with all our hearts.***

***

I have learned to serve Him with the gifts and talents He has given me, even when they don't align with people's expectations. I have been told I had to serve through music, because, as a chaplain's wife, many people assume I sing or play the piano. When we first moved to Germany, I was informed I would be part of the "chaplain's wives singing group." I laughed at these ladies. I told them I did not (and still don't) sing. I cannot carry a tune or play any instruments, but I volunteered to hold up applause signs if that would help. They did not believe me. One of their husbands even called my husband and told him I had missed practice. Dave laughed and said, "Have you heard my wife sing?" They wanted me to serve my Adonai differently than I am gifted.

Asking me to be a part of a singing group would be like asking a servant who is in charge of the stables to come into the kitchen to make dinner or telling a chef to go tend to the horses. I can still make a joyful noise, but being part of a praise team is not how Adonai has equipped me to serve Him. He has instead gifted me with the skills to teach, lead, and administrate.

***

***Adonai wants His bondservants to serve Him
as He has created and gifted them.***

***

He calls us all to serve, but He has not given us all the same gifts for doing so.

> *Now there are varieties of gifts, but the same Spirit; and there are varieties of service, but the same Lord; and there are varieties of activities, but it is the same God who empowers them all in everyone. To each is given the manifestation of the Spirit for the common good. For to one is given through the Spirit the utterance of wisdom, and to another the utterance of knowledge according to the same Spirit, to another faith by the same Spirit, to another gifts of healing by the one Spirit, to another the working of miracles, to another prophecy, to another the ability to distinguish between spirits, to another various kinds of tongues, to another the interpretation of tongues. All these are empowered by one and the same Spirit, who apportions to each one individually as he wills.* 1 Corinthians 12:4-11

God wants us to serve in our gifts. When we don't serve in our gifts, we will wear ourselves out. We will work and work and not feel at peace. I have worked outside my talents when I tried to do the outreach position in a military women's ministry program. Outreach means organizing things to reach out to the people around the base. When I served in that position, it did not go well. When someone else organized and planned it, we met the needs of people. Another time when I was the Spiritual Life Vice President, I had to display the Bible study books for the semester. I laid them out in rows on a table with sign-up sheets. I thought it was fine, but my friend who loves to "foof" (make things look beautiful) came along and pulled out different things to make it look great. She laughed with me at my ineptitude. She can "foof," but I can teach. These experiences taught me that I don't need to say yes just because people ask. I need to wait on God and work within my gifts.

***

Adonai wants us to serve Him with all our hearts in order to build up the body of believers of which we are all a part.

***

Each of us is needed to serve God, but we need to remain on the mission He has chosen us for. Does that mean that God doesn't change our gifts? No, sometimes He changes or adds to our gifts. He wants us to keep growing to become better bondservants.

Now you are the body of Christ and individually members of it. And God has appointed in the church, first apostles, second prophets, third teachers, then miracles, then gifts of healings, helping, administrating, various

> *kinds of tongues. Are all apostles? Are all prophets? Are all teachers? Do all work miracles? Do all possess gifts of healing? Do all speak with tongues? Do all interpret? But earnestly desire the higher gifts. And I will show you a still more excellent way.* 1 Corinthians 12:27-31

When I was in High School, my Campus Life Club director joked about people being part of the body. He would label himself or someone else as an arm or a foot or the nose. I always wanted to be the feet or hands of the body. Instead, they called me the "MOB — Mouth of the Body." One of my gifts is a loud voice that can be heard in most large rooms. I often only have to say one word before people turn to look at me and stop talking. I guess Adonai likes me as the MOB. It helped when I was a high school teacher, so I don't mind.

Yet, Adonai wants us to do everything in love. I must be careful when I use my loud voice because some people do not appreciate it. I use it when asked but have grown sensitive to people who don't appreciate it. Adonai is the Lord and Master of my voice. Adonai will lead if I let Him lead me. We are also to make sure that we are serving in the fruit of the Spirit as described in the book of Galatians.

> *But the fruit of the Spirit is love, joy, peace, patience, kindness, goodness, faithfulness, gentleness, self-control; against such things there is no law. And those who belong to Christ Jesus have crucified the flesh with its passions and desires. If we live by the Spirit, let us also keep in step with the Spirit. Let us not become conceited, provoking one another, envying one another.* Galatians 5:22-26

As we serve Adonai, we need to make sure the fruit of the Spirit shines through. We don't get part of the list. We have all of it. We should show love, joy, peace, patience, kindness, goodness, faithfulness, gentleness, and self-control as we go about every mission Adonai assigns us.

Queen Elizabeth's servants show many of these characteristics even if they don't love her. They have self-control, gentleness, faithfulness, patience, and appear to be at peace in the public eye. I don't know if they act out in private, but in public they are very reserved. I wish I could be like them, because I often fail to display the full fruit of the Spirit. I often fail to act with patience or gentleness when I'm stressed out or in a hurry. My extra weight shows I don't have self-control and my face doesn't radiate joy all the time. As I have focused more and more on Adonai, I have noticed how He brings out the fruit in me. He will change us because He wants us to grow under His leadership.

Adonai wants and deserves to be Lord and Master over all parts of our lives. When we give Him our hearts, He will guide us. Through our prayers, we can learn from Him and join other believers in His throne room praising and worshiping Him. Adonai, Our Lord and Master, deserves our praise, our worship, and our service. Serving Him will show His love to all the people around you. Adonai is our Lord and Master; He calls us into His throne room, which we will learn about in our next chapter.

Prayer to Adonai   (adapted from Psalm 148)

Praise the Lord!
Praise Adonai from the heavens;
Praise Him in the heights!
Praise Him, all His angels;
Praise Him, all His hosts!

Praise Him, sun and moon,
praise Him, all you shining stars!
Praise Him, you highest heavens,
and you waters above the heavens!

Let them praise the name of Adonai!
For He commanded, and they were created.
And He established them forever and ever;
He gave a decree, and it shall not pass away.

Praise Adonai from the earth,
you great sea creatures and all deeps,
fire and hail, snow and mist,
stormy wind fulfilling His word!

Mountains and all hills,
fruit trees and all cedars!
Beasts and all livestock,
creeping things and flying birds!

Kings of the earth and all peoples,
princes and all rulers of the earth!
Young men and maidens together,
old men and children!

Let them praise the name of Adonai,
for His name alone is exalted;
His majesty is above earth and heaven.
He has raised up a horn for His people,
praise for all His saints who are near to Him.
Praise the Lord. Amen

Questions for Discussion

These questions can be used for personal study or for group discussion.

1. Have you become a bondservant to Adonai? What does that term mean to you? What do you believe a bondservant does?

2. How do you show Adonai that He is your Lord?

3. Why is it important to focus on Adonai as your Master and Lord?

4. When in your life did you not follow God?

5. How would you describe your life away from Adonai? How is it different when you serve Adonai?

6. In Exodus 6:3, God speaks to Moses and says that He did not show Himself as Adonai to Abraham, Isaac, and Jacob. Why do you think He said that to Moses? Why is that important?

7. As a bondservant, how has Adonai gifted you with skills or talents to serve Him and accomplish your mission?

8. How will your increased understanding of God as Adonai, empower you in God's mission? Write out a prayer to Adonai claiming the promises and character of God indicated by this Call Sign.

Notes:

4. EL ELYON: THE LORD MOST HIGH

As daughters of El Elyon, we have the privilege of entering His throne room with our petitions.

As I looked into God's Call Sign, El Elyon, I was drawn to the concept of fearing God. El means high. Elyon means most high. So El Elyon literally means highest of high. This means that El Elyon is the highest God there is. He is all-powerful (omnipotent). He is more than anything else. He is perfect. He has no sin in Him. He is the final authority.

Fearing God is the beginning of Wisdom. Fear God. What does it mean to "fear God?" What does that look like? How do I fear God? Why do I need to fear Him? Isn't God also Abba Father? Do I fear my father? Should I fear my father? Yet what does this have to do with fearing God? These questions made it clear that I needed to understand what the "fear of God" truly means.

The fear of God is oftentimes explained as respecting God, but I think this is too shallow. To fear God is to understand our relationship with Him. He creates us, He controls everything. He is all-powerful. We need to truly fear His power, His justice, and His wrath. God destroyed the world with the flood but He spared

53

Noah's family. He destroyed Sodom and Gomorrah and toppled the Tower of Babel, causing men to speak different languages. His Will is never thwarted. He holds everything in His hand. He is so powerful.

In Exodus, Moses wants proof of God's glory:

> *And the LORD said to Moses, "This very thing that you have spoken I will do, for you have found favor in my sight, and I know you by name." Moses said, "Please show me your glory." ^{19}And he said, "I will make all my goodness pass before you, and will proclaim before you my name, 'the LORD.' And I will be gracious to whom I will be gracious, and will show mercy on whom I will show mercy. But," he said, "you cannot see my face, for man shall not see me and live." And the LORD said, "Behold, there is a place by me where you shall stand on a rock, and while my glory passes by I will put you in a cleft of the rock and I will cover you with my hand until I have passed by. Then I will take away my hand and you will see my back; but my face shall not be seen."*
> Exodus 33:17-23

Moses, who could talk to God and spend time with Him, could not see God's face because it would destroy him. Moses realized that El Elyon was beyond everything so he bowed to the ground and worshiped Him. God is amazing and powerful. We are to fear Him, yet because we are His daughters, He grants us entrance into his throne room through our prayers.

In Psalm 111:10, the psalmist writes, "The fear of the LORD is the beginning of wisdom; all those who practice it have a good understanding. His praise endures forever!" Proverbs 1:7 states, "The fear of the LORD is the beginning of knowledge; fools despise wisdom and instruction." We must start our journey towards God with the right attitude.

Our sins cause our separation from God. He is perfect and we are not. That is why Jesus had to die. He died to take away our sins so we can enter into El Elyon's presence.

> *"When I saw him, I fell at His feet as though dead. But he laid his right hand on me, saying, "Fear not, I am the first and the last, and the living one. I died, and behold, I am alive forevermore, and I have the keys of Death and Hades." Revelation 1:17-18*

God has sent His Son to die for us to give us a loving relationship with El Elyon. We don't have to fear the future because He has sent Jesus to save us. He has provided Christ to bridge the gap between us and El Elyon.

God is so awesome and amazing that everything and everyone will bow down to Him. Look in Revelation; the priests and angels serve Him and bow before Him. He is El Elyon, the Lord Most High. Nothing is greater. He is worthy of all worship and praise. Because of this greatness, we should fear His power and His might. At His Word, things are created and destroyed. This Call Sign reminds us of His might and power.

God told Moses to remove his sandals when El Elyon spoke to him because he was standing on holy ground. Wherever El Elyon is, that is holy ground. El Elyon also put His hand over Moses to protect him as He passed by. Without this protection, El Elyon's greatness would have destroyed Moses. After Moses spent time with El Elyon, Moses' face shone like a bride on her wedding day. The Israelites realized some of El Elyon's greatness had touched Moses so they made him cover his face until it disappeared. The Israelites understood El Elyon is so much greater, He is worthy to be feared and worshipped. But even they forgot from time to time. We read throughout the Old Testament about how the Nation of Israel's success and failure hinged on how God's character influences their king's mission.

Since we live in New Testament times, many people believe fearing God is no longer necessary. But Scripture clearly says fear of the Lord is the beginning of wisdom. I believe we need to fear God because of who He is, El Elyon. But El Elyon is full of grace, love, and mercy. Christ stands between El Elyon and us. We could never be in El Elyon's presence due to our sins. He is so much greater than we can imagine. But because Christ died for our sins, He sits beside God intervening for us, shielding us from the Father's wrath so that we might have the privilege of coming before Him.

***

As daughters of El Elyon, we have the privilege of entering His throne room with our repentance.

***

I like to think of Christ standing between El Elyon and me with his arms outstretched saying, "Yes, Jennifer sinned again, but her judgment is on me." I am bowing down with my head on the ground and then I feel El Elyon call me and say, "Jennifer you are forgiven." I then stand up and rejoice with all the rest of the saints in the throne room of God.

During my time here on earth, remembering God's Call Sign, El Elyon, helps me. Fear of His wrath makes me think before sinning. Many times I don't stop, but sometimes I do. El Elyon reminds me of the stories of the kings of the Old Testament. People would go to the palace to have an audience with the king. When they went before the king, they would bow with their heads to the ground. They would not dare raise so much as an eyebrow until the king permitted it.

Look at the book of Esther. The king was unhappy with his current queen so he decided to find another. He did not kill his queen, nor did he divorce her. Instead, she was no longer allowed to come into the presence of the king (Esther 1:19). This makes me think about how my sin makes me unclean so I cannot enter into the presence of El Elyon.

But the king was lonely so he sent out men to all the areas to gather beautiful young virgins. Esther was a beautiful young virgin so she was taken from her family and put into the harem to be prepared to meet the king. After the year-long preparation, she went to the king and then was moved to the harem of concubines. Esther found favor with the king so he made her queen. She was honored and blessed by the people of the court. Yet she could not see the king unless he called for her.

She was queen, yet still could not see the king without his permission. Read that again, she was the queen, yet still could not see the king without his permission. This made me stop. In today's society, men and women are equal. Yet not in a monarchy. Right now there is no King of England. We have a Queen but no king. She is married but her husband is not called king. This is from laws enacted long ago. Kings have more power than queens. So the Queen can't have a King. Her son Crown Prince Charles will become King of England and then his wife will become the queen. There are so many rules and laws governing monarchies. People cannot just talk to the king or queen without permission.

El Elyon is the High King. He is perfect. We cannot enter His courts without permission. The blood of Christ gives us permission to enter the throne room. Christ's blood is our cleansing. He washed away our sins so that El Elyon can welcome us into His presence.

***

As daughters of El Elyon, we have the privilege of entering His throne room with our robes washed white by the blood of Christ.
***

Esther had to enter the king's presence without permission to save her own life and the lives of her people. I wonder if she thought about Psalm 57:2; "I will cry to God Most High, to God who accomplishes *all things* for me." Only El Elyon could stop the king from banishing her or killing her. El Elyon softened the king's heart toward Esther and allowed her to live and invite the king to dinner. El Elyon saved her own life and the lives of her people. She trusted El Elyon's authority enough to carry out the mission He had given her, even though it could have cost her her life. Her fear of El Elyon exceeded her fear of the king.

I need to remember Psalm 9:2: "I will be glad and exult in you; I will sing praise to your name, O Most High." El Elyon has proven himself to me time and again. Sometimes the proof is easier to see in hindsight.

As I look back at my post-college, pre-marriage days, El Elyon's hand was very evident. While in college, I did not grow very close to El Elyon. I went to church but that was about it. When I could not find a teaching position in New York near my family and friends, El Elyon gave me one in Martinsburg, West Virginia. Far from home, I was scared. I cried out to El Elyon to help me, and He brought me the comfort and confidence I needed to carry on in the book of Psalms. Psalm 78:35 says, "They remembered that God was their rock, the Most High God their Redeemer." El Elyon is my rock. This verse reminded me that El Elyon and Jesus are one and the same. God is the Father, the Son, and the Holy Spirit. They are one. El Elyon is not separate from our Redeemer. Not only is El Elyon the Most High God, but he also loves me enough to plant me on solid ground and buy me back from the grips of the enemy. The One who holds the whole world in His hands cares about every detail of my life. He knows where I will live, how I will get there, who I will meet when I arrive. He cares about my heart's desires for my family, friends, the mission He has given me, and rest.

I can see both His control and care in every detail of my move to West Virginia. First, He led me to Peachy, who worked at the school board. She took me in and stayed with her for several months, despite the fact that her husband had recently passed and she had two small children. She found me an apartment, encouraged me to go to church, and constantly prayed with me and for me. El Elyon wanted me to learn about Him, so He used this dear woman whose faith did not waver even when faced with the death of her beloved husband. She taught me about El Elyon and His perfect love. He also sent me a friend named Wendy, who met with me weekly for Bible study and discipleship. Because these women trusted God as Lord Most High and accepted their mission to make Him known throughout the world, I started to grow as a Christian.

I lived in Martinsburg for two years and thought I knew everything. But of course, El Elyon knew better. In nearly Job-like fashion, He took away my car (engine trouble), then my apartment (leaking roof), then my job (they wanted me to teach seven periods a day without any breaks after I left they hired two teachers to do my job). I was lost. I did not know what to do. My friend Wendy said, "You need to leave here and go to Virginia." I did not know anyone there. Yet, El Elyon was in control of all of it.

Just to make sure I knew who was in control, everything about my move to Virginia was opposite what the world said to do. First, I got a new car. I had no job or place to live but a new car. Then, El Elyon gave me a house. Without a job, the landlord let me rent the house. Next, El Elyon sent two Christian roommates to help with expenses. Finally, He gave me a job just down the road teaching Chemistry and Physics. El Elyon, The Lord Most High, wanted to show me who was in control by doing things in a way that defied human logic.

One of my roommates, Jodi, helped me find my first church "home." When I was in West Virginia, I went to church but it never felt like home. In Virginia, Jodi told me about Burke Community Church. I went and fell in love with the people and spirit of the church. I truly felt like I was "home." El Elyon gave me my spiritual mom, Ruth. She taught me about prayer and how to study the Bible. We met for many years, and it was such a wonderful time of growth for me. The Lord Most High knew I needed to learn and grow. He knew the right church for me. I stayed in Virginia for six years and met my husband there. El Elyon knew what I needed and when I needed it.

When we approach El Elyon, we need to have the right kind of fear but also trust in Jesus. Because of trusting in our Savior, we are saved. We need to understand the great and awesome nature of El Elyon. Without Jesus saving us, we are not allowed to enter into the presence of El Elyon.

El Elyon is in control of everything. When we enter into His presence on our knees in prayer He blesses us. He is not going to give us everything we want. Instead, He will show us what we need to grow closer to Him and ultimately fulfill our mission to make God the Lord Most High known in all the places He sends us. Deuteronomy 10:17 states, "For the Lord, your God is God of gods and Lord of Lords, the great, the mighty, and the awesome God, who is not partial and takes no bribe." We cannot convince Him nor bribe Him to do things. He is in control and His commission will be done.

Jesus taught us about this in what we call The Lord's Prayer found in Matthew 6:9-15. Jesus taught people to pray, "Your kingdom come, Your will be done, on earth as it is in heaven." El Elyon's kingdom will come to earth someday. He will be praised by all and prove Himself to be the Lord Most High.

Through all His Call Signs, God continues to show me many facets of His character. He is El Elyon the Lord Most High. He is mighty, omnipotent, omnipresent, omniscient, and He sees everything. Nothing is hidden from Him. He knows everything, yet loves us. Nothing can separate us from His love. When God moves you to a new place, a new job, or a new season of life, He does not leave you there alone. El Elyon is with you through every change, every trial, and every tear. He has created you for a mission that only you can fulfill. Your mission may be raising kids, it may be working full time or it could be both at the same time. El Elyon is with you and will strengthen you and encourage you. He is with you; He sees what you focus on and is jealous of your time, which brings us to the next to last Call Sign—El Qanna.

Prayer to El Elyon (adapted from Psalm 91)

*I dwell in the shelter of **El Elyon**,*
will abide in the shadow of El Shaddai.
I will say to the LORD, *"You are My refuge and my fortress, my God, in whom I trust!"*

For El Elyon will deliver me from the plans of the devil and from the deadly illnesses.
You will protect me during the battles I face.
You watch over me day and night.

El Elyon will cover me with His feathers, and under His wings, I will find refuge;
His faithfulness is a shield and rampart.

I will not fear the terror of the night, nor of the arrow that flies by day;
nor the pestilence that stalks in darkness,
nor the destruction that lays wastes at noonday.
I will not fear deployments, separations, time alone. I will not fear the world around me because El Elyon is with me.

A thousand may fall at my side, ten thousand at my right hand,
but it will not come near me.
I will only look with your eyes and see the recompense of the wicked.

Because I have made the LORD *my dwelling place-El Elyon, who is my refuge--*
no evil will be allowed to befall me, no plague will come near my tent.

For El Elyon will command His angels concerning me to guard me in all my ways.
On their hands, they will bear me up, lest I strike my foot against a stone.
I will tread on the lion and the snake;
the young lion and the serpent I will trample underfoot.

El Elyon says, "Because she holds fast to Me in love, I will deliver her;
I will protect her because she knows My name.
When she calls to me, I will answer her; I will be with her in trouble;
I will rescue her and honor her.
With long life, I will satisfy her and show her My salvation." Amen

Questions for Discussion

These questions can be used for personal study or for group discussion.

1. Reflect on the statement: "El Elyon is in control of everything." Give an example of how He is in control of a specific area of your life.

2. What does the fear of the Lord mean to you? How do you fear the Lord?

3. When have you seen El Elyon's character displayed in the Bible? What stories come to mind?

4. How do you see El Elyon in the book of Ruth?

5. What does El Elyon do in the book of Job?

6. Meditate on Psalm 78:35. What does this verse mean to you?

7. Hebrews 7 retells the story of Abraham meeting Melchizedek. How do you see El Elyon in this story?

8. What area(s) of your life do you need to give to El Elyon? Write actions that could help you surrender that area to God.

9. Read Matthew 6:9-15. What Call Signs do you see in these verses?

10. How will your increased understanding of God as El Elyon, empower you to fulfill God's mission for you? Write out a prayer to El Elyon claiming the promises and character of God indicated by this Call Sign.

Notes:

5. *EL QANNA: THE LORD IS JEALOUS*

El Qanna desires us with His eternal Love.

My God is El Qanna, meaning the King is jealous. This Call Sign for God can be difficult for many people to accept and understand. We have been taught that jealousy can hurt human relationships. When people become jealous, they often make poor decisions and say things that hurt others. Oprah Winfrey has said she gave up on being a Christian because of the teachings about God being El Qanna.

> With Tolle as a guest, Oprah explains how her view of God and the spiritual teachings of Christianity changed in her late 20's after hearing a preacher describe God as a 'jealous' God. She said that by

opening her mind to the "hugeness" of God, she was able to accept the notion that God is not jealous, but rather a "God of love."[1]

"Oprah told a personal story from her Baptist upbringing during which she was in church (around the age of 27 or 28 years of age) and was caught up in the rapture of the moment until she heard her Pastor say, "The Lord thy God is a jealous God. Oprah's immediate inward response was, "God is jealous of me?" It was then Oprah began searching for something more remembering that God is love, omnipresent, and omniscient. "I asked God to use me, that has been my prayer for many years," Oprah conveyed.[2]

Many people who listen to Oprah agree with her ideas. However, if she had looked into the Scriptures she would have learned about El Qanna. I sometimes jump to conclusions during a sermon but God always brings me back to His Word. Oprah took the passage totally out of context. This idea of El Qanna is found in several passages.

> *You shall not bow down to them or serve them, for I, the LORD your God, am a **jealous God**, visiting the iniquity of the fathers on the children to the third and the fourth generations of those who hate me*, Exodus 20:5

> *—for you shall worship no other god, for the LORD, whose name is **Jealous (El Qanna)**, is a **jealous God**.* Exodus 34:14

> *You shall not bow down to them or serve them; for I the LORD your God, am a **jealous God**, visiting the iniquity of the fathers on the children to the third and the fourth generations of those who hate me*, Deuteronomy 5:9

***
El Qanna is not jealous of us.
***

Rest assured; God is perfect. He may be jealous, but He will never make poor decisions or say things that unnecessarily hurt people. He is jealous of our love of other things. He is jealous of when we worship other things like money, food, technology, relationships, anything which takes our devotions away from Him. When I spend time on the computer checking Facebook or reading emails in moments when I know I should be with God, I believe He is El Qanna. He wants time with me. He wants me to learn about Him, to pray, to spend time with Him. He is jealous for my love, my time, my focus, and my devotion.

El Qanna does not want our rote prayers or our Sunday worship. He wants us to talk to Him and tell Him all our thoughts, hopes, dreams, fears, and worries.

***

He wants us to tell Him everything.
***

He convicts me of this when I share my feelings with my friends before I share them with God. I want to vent so I turn to people instead of turning to El Qanna. Sharing with friends or family is not bad in and of itself. What is wrong is when we turn to people and ignore God. God wants us to tell Him all of our life. He knows everything going on in our hearts, minds, and bodies but He wants us to share it with Him as an act of trust that deepens our relationship with Him. When we have spent at least a year at a duty station, I start wondering/worrying about moving and losing friends. I am often tempted to preemptively turn away from friends because I don't want to experience the pain of leaving them. Do I turn toward God instead? Sometimes. I try to remind myself to turn towards Him to share my heart with Him. El Qanna loves when we share our hearts with Him so He can hold us and comfort us.

When we share our hearts with Him, it opens us up to the vulnerability of not knowing how He will work things out in our various situations. Oftentimes I find myself praying, "Your will be done," while thinking "but I really want it this way," my way. I have learned to tell Him what I want but then I also pray for His perfect will and plan to be done. When I share my heart and do not hold things back, I gain peace and release my worries. Yet, I also want His will and His plan in His time, not mine. Sometimes my heart's desire is in line with His plan, sometimes not.

When I was forced to stop with my broken leg, Jehovah-Jireh provided everything beyond what I could imagine. One of the ways He provided for me was through my wonderful husband who thought of all my needs and desires. He set up a TV and a DVD player and gave me movies to watch. I enjoyed that for a few days but then El Qanna crashed into my thoughts. He wanted me to work on this book and not watch TV for hours on end. Most shows and movies became irritating to me. I knew He wanted me to spend time with Him. El Qanna was jealous that I focused on a man-made show instead of the Creator of men. Because of this irritation, I started to write this book. Even now when I am supposed to be studying or listening and I am tempted to do other things. El Qanna bothers me until I focus on Him and not on the world. I don't always turn to Him but He constantly wants me to focus on Him.

***
El Qanna wants us to focus on His character.
***

Sunday worship can be a source of jealousy. We go into worship, excited about the praise and worship team. We often idolize them instead of focusing on El Qanna. El Qanna desires us to praise Him and worship Him, not the pastor, the building, the praise and worship team, or any other part of our worship time.

As an Army chaplain's wife, I am blessed to hear many preachers. Some draw you into Scripture so you want to learn more about El Qanna. Others tell story after story so the point of the sermon is lost. I think El Qanna wants our Sunday church time to be about learning from the Scriptures. He wants us to focus on learning about Him, not about what people are wearing or if the singing is perfect. I often forget to focus on Him because I am socializing and greeting instead of preparing to worship Him. If I am honest, I am also comparing myself to others, judging them, and judging myself.

El Qanna wants us to spend time with Him. He wants us to spend time daily with Him. When I was a young believer, I was told to have a daily "Quiet Time" with God. I had no idea what a "Quiet Time" was. So, I started reading the Bible. Like most new believers, without guidance, I went to the beginning of the Bible and started reading. By Exodus, I quit. I reasoned God could not be this boring. Starting in the Book of John or one of the other Gospels would have been much better. Instead, after the Creation story, I became lost in genealogy and occasional stories I remembered from Sunday School.

It took me decades to learn how to study the Bible on my own. I needed to have a plan when I was learning about God. Because El Qanna wants me to spend time studying His Word, I have learned to study the Bible. When I start a book, I spend time researching who wrote it, when, what was going on at that time, and the genre of the writing. Then, I read it slowly, usually a chapter a day looking for why God placed it in the Bible. Some of the books in the Old Testament are still challenging, but little by little, day by day, I learn more about the love of El Qanna.

***
Time with El Qanna's Word brings us closer to Him.
***

El Qanna also wants my prayer time. Prayer is a time to tell God what is going on, your heart, your pain, your honesty, and then any requests. However, it also MUST be a time to be still and listen to God. He is jealous for our listening, too. We tend to listen to the world easily but forget to listen to Him. He wants us to listen for His still small voice.

I often find myself distracted by the activity of getting kids out the door in the morning. I try to get up earlier but I find myself thinking about sleep. Doing my "Quiet Time" takes discipline and hard work. I have to carve out time and focus. I find walking my dog often allows me to focus on Adonai, my Lord and Master. I pray for everyone He brings to mind. When I return home, I do my El Shaddai yoga. Then I dive into the Scriptures to see what God wants to reveal to me.

The time of day you spend with God is between you and God. My time with God will be different than your time with God. God wants our time; He will show us how and when to do it. When I had little kids, my time with God was often praying at the kitchen sink or while doing laundry, any time I could take a second and pray or listen to a praise and worship song. My kids are older now so my time is more my own, but that does not mean it is any easier. I would rather procrastinate and check Facebook many mornings, but I've found I'm less likely to spend time in His presence if I don't do it early in the day. El Qanna wants time with me daily. The time of day does not matter; what is important is having time with El Qanna.

El Qanna is Elohim, the Creator of everything. He is not jealous of us. He is jealous for our time, energy, and focus. He has everything, He owns the sheep on a thousand hills. He created and gave us everything we have. What He desires is for us to have fellowship with Him. Don't fall into the trap of the world which says we are the most important things. God created us. When we die, the world does not stop. I learned of my unimportance when I had to sit and heal. The world around me continued, meetings continued, Protestant Women Of the Chapel continued to grow, my family could clean a house, and the list goes on. I was not indispensable.

God is jealous when we put ourselves up as being indispensable. Especially life in the military shows us, we can be replaced. The people who replace us may do things differently, but that is not bad. When we are called to stop doing something El Qanna wants us to obey and not hold onto the thing no matter how important that mission may seem. Holding on to a ministry or a job after God calls you away from it causes your focus to be turned from God. Because the Army tells us to move, I often have to give up ministry positions. Sometimes I do it at the correct time, which is when God tells me. Other times I drag my feet a little too long.

When I spend time with the LORD, I learn what to give up. I love being involved in the community wherever God moves us. Yet, many who know me maybe surprised, I am an introvert. So, when I spend a great deal of time with other people, I lose energy. God knows this, and He will want me to say no to commitments, but I often find it hard to say no. He calls me, gently or other times more loudly, and asks me to stop, step away from people, and spend time with Him. When I spend time with Him, I gain peace, rest, and strength. When I refuse, I feel El Qanna becoming more insistent. He wants me to be selective with my time and my focus.

***
When I put El Qanna first,
I am more successful, peaceful, and encouraged.
***

Many people talk about healthy priorities. I strive to place God first, my husband second, my kids third, then everything else. If I choose to get things out of order, El Qanna will remind me of what is important...Him. He has removed me from ministry many times because of my misplaced priorities.

In Texas, He called me out of Protestant Women Of the Chapel, because it had become my idol. During my recovery time for my leg, the only day I could get physical therapy or a doctor's appointment for my ankle was on Tuesdays. This was when PWOC met. Every PWOC day would be the only time I could get an appointment. This went on for three months until I stopped fighting Him and admitted my idolatry of this ministry. He allowed me to return about a month before summer started. And by His Grace, His timing allowed me to make friends yet not apply to serve on the board.

Over the years, He has removed me from a variety of activities. Coaching young kids, substitute teaching, and volunteering to do taxes; each of these activities were for a season. Many times, when I have said yes, before I prayed, He did not give me rest or peace about my decision. I have had to swallow my pride and correct my commitments. If I don't agree to a commitment, He wants me to do, He will also bother me. Being an introvert, I sometimes say no when He wants me to say yes. I have learned when I struggle to be successful, lack peace, or feel discouraged, I need to call on God according to His Call Sign El Qanna. He has never failed to meet my need for divine discernment regarding mission assignments or time management when I seek Him first.

God will use His Word to teach us and train us. He wants us to learn using His Word. There have been many times when Scripture rebuked me. He speaks through His Word. Some verses in the Bible can seem harsh, but they are in the Bible to teach us and correct us.

> *"All Scripture is breathed out by God and profitable for teaching, for reproof, for correction, and for training in righteousness, that the man of God may be complete, equipped for every good work.* 2 Timothy 3:16-17

After my original Bible reading failure in Exodus, I spent most of my time studying the New Testament. As I grew closer to God, He took me back to the Old Testament. The Old Testament can be very confusing, but God inspired me to study the Bible Chronologically so I could see how parts of the Old Testament related to each other and the whole story. This really helped me get over my fear of the Old Testament. Since then, I have enjoyed seeing the richness in the Old Testament and how God intertwines all the books.

Through my reading of the Old Testament, I found El Qanna in many stories. El Qanna met Moses in the desert and called Moses to lead His people out of Egypt. He sent a messenger in the form of a burning bush that was not consumed (Exodus 3:2-6). El Qanna called Moses because He was jealous for His people to return to the Promised Land. El Qanna can also mean, "consuming fire." He will ultimately destroy all things that are not holy. He is the fire by which we are purified as seen in Psalm 66:10: "For You have tried us, O God (Elohim); You have refined us as silver is refined." El Qanna will purify us by casting out our sins and every idol that distracts us from Him.

When you heat silver, the impurities float to the surface. This is called "dross", and silversmiths scoop this from the surface of the silver. After this is done several times, the surface of the silver will become like a mirror showing the reflection of the silversmith, meaning the silver is pure. This is the process El Qanna describes in Psalm 66:10. He wants to take away all our impurities and make us a perfect reflection of Himself. He wants us to show the world His perfect love through the missions He gives us to serve our neighbors.
In the book of Joshua, Joshua talks to the people about serving God.

> *But Joshua said to the people, "You are not able to serve the LORD, for he is a holy God. He is a jealous God* **(El Qanna)***; he will not forgive your transgression or your sins. If you forsake the LORD and serve foreign gods, then he will turn and do you harm and consume you, after having done you good." And the people said to Joshua, "No, but we will serve the LORD." Then Joshua said to the people, "You are witnesses against yourselves that you have chosen the Lord, to serve Him." And they said, "We are witnesses." He said, "Then put away the foreign gods that are in among you, and incline your hearts to the LORD, the God of Israel." And the people said to Joshua, "The Lord our God we will serve, and his voice we will obey."*
> Joshua 24:19-24

Joshua did not believe the people would pursue God at all costs, so he repeatedly asked if they truly were going to follow God. They said yes with their mouths but the stories recorded in later years proved their hearts could not stay true to their promises. People today are no different. I promise to follow God or do daily "Quiet Time" or pray without ceasing, yet I forget and fall away.

The more often I fall away, the more likely I am to fall prey to the newest fad. One of Satan's most popular new tools is "tolerance." According to the Merriam-Webster dictionary, "tolerance is sympathy or indulgence for beliefs or practices different from or conflicting with one's own."[3] People use today's tolerance fad to try to force people to change their beliefs to align with their own. I have been called intolerant because I stand on the Word of God. God's Truth is capital T truth, meaning it does not change. If I am brave enough to admit I don't agree with a person's beliefs because they don't follow God's Truth, I am considered intolerant or ignorant. Tolerance does not mean changing my beliefs, it means allowing other people to have their own beliefs. I pray for these people and ask God to give me words to change their minds but I try not to attack them.

Today's world does not want right and wrong. It wants everything to be accepted by everybody which leads to evil. Satan loves grey areas. Right and wrong are hard to argue with but if we change even a word then right and wrong are harder to see. Look at Eve in the Garden, she changed what God said which led to the fall. El Qanna is jealous for people to do what is right in His sight and avoid the temptations of their own flesh to do wrong.

One Sunday as worship began, vacation planning consumed my mind and distracted my heart. We started singing and I was not in the mindset to worship. Chapel service became just another thing to check off on my very long to-do list. Missing chapel was not an option, but my heart was not ready to worship God.

El Qanna got my attention with a song by the David Crowder Band: **"How He Loves"**

> He is jealous for me, Loves like a hurricane, I am a tree,
> Bending beneath the weight of his wind and mercy.[4]

El Qanna is the name God uses to show us how much He loves us. He is jealous for us over everything. He loves like a hurricane. As trees bend beneath the wind of a hurricane, you can tell the healthy trees from the rotten and brittle ones.

Pine trees surrounded our house, in South Carolina. These trees are tall and thin for the most part. One morning I walked out to see one of the pines leaning over. It looked healthy from the outside, but the roots sticking out of the ground were very shallow. I called a tree service and the owner said most pine trees have shallow roots. I was surprised since South Carolina can get hurricanes, yet there are pine trees everywhere. He said, "In a forest, pine trees can withstand a hurricane by supporting each other. Without the support of other pine trees, any strong wind, let alone a hurricane, will topple pine trees easily."

The lyrics to "**How He Loves**" talk about bending beneath the weight of His wind, (power) and mercy. I need to remember to bend and not try to go it alone. If I stand alone, I will topple over. I need to dig my roots down into God's Word and fellowship, so I can grow strong and withstand the storms of life.

As we look at God, He is truly El Qanna. He is Jealous. He wants us to give up everything to serve Him, sometimes even our families. Luke 9 relates Jesus' travel to Jerusalem with His disciples and other followers. He speaks to them in the following verses:

> *To another he said, "Follow Me." But he said, "Lord, let me first go and bury my father." And Jesus said to him, "Leave the dead to bury their own dead. But as for you, go and proclaim the kingdom of God." Yet another said, "I will follow you, Lord, but let me first say farewell to those at my home." Jesus said to him, "No one, who puts his hand to the plow and looks back is fit for the kingdom of God."Luke 9:59-62*

He also challenged His disciples with the idea that their work would lead to more separations and sacrifice.

> *Jesus said, "Truly, I say to you, there is no one who has left house or brothers or sisters or mother or father or children or lands, for my sake and for the gospel, who will not receive a hundredfold now in this time, houses and brothers and sisters and mothers and children and lands, with persecutions, and in the age to come, eternal life. But many who are first will be last, and the last, first."Mark 10:29-31*

Jesus talked about sacrificing everything, but this wasn't just an empty exhortation; He gave up everything for us. He wants us to give up everything to follow Him. When my kids were little, a pastor challenged the congregation to give their children to God. At the time, I did not envision this as difficult, but now as I have grown in understanding I see how challenging it is.

El Qanna wants me to give my children to Him, because He is jealous for them, too. I am trying to be ok with allowing El Qanna to plan and direct their paths and futures, but it is hard. "What if you send them into danger? What happens if they get sick? What happens if they die?" These questions circle around in my mind whenever I pray over my children and their futures. This assumes I can help them all the time. I need to try to give them to God instead of holding on to them. This is a daily challenge for me. As a mother, I want only the best for them, yet I think I know the best when, in reality, only God knows the plans and missions He has for them.

God taught me with my first child that wanting the best means disciplining them. Many times, it would have been easier to let my children have their way, but they would not have learned self-control or patience. I look back now and realize I often act more like a two-year-old than a grown woman. I stomp my feet at God and want my own way. El Qanna does not allow me to act out without correction. He works in our lives to teach us so much.

> *"For this very reason, make every effort to supplement your faith with virtue, and virtue with knowledge, and knowledge with self-control, and self-control with steadfastness, and steadfastness with godliness; and godliness with brotherly affection; and brotherly affection with love."*
> 2 Peter 1:5-7

El Qanna wants us to grow in all of His qualities--patience, faith, love, self-control, and so many more. He is jealous of whatever competes with our time with Him, shifts our focus from Him, or shapes our lives in the image of anything not like Him. He wants us to spend time with Him and learn from Him, so we can become more like Him. When we are tired of fighting and His kneading us to change, Abba will hold us to replenish us. We can call on God according to His Call Sign, El Qanna. He empowers us to accomplish our mission by putting Him first in our lives.

Prayer to El Qanna

El Qanna thank you for forgiving me for constantly finding idols. I worship money and material things. I focus on making money rather than giving you the first ten percent of it. Instead of tithing, I hold tight to my money out of fear or because I love it more than you.

My house and all my possessions are yours. You have given me everything. When I move I worry about the movers and what will happen to my things. Instead of trusting you, I worry about losing things or things being damaged or destroyed. I idolize my things rather than focusing on you and how you provide more than I can imagine.

My children are the center of my life. I love them so much. As they grow do I allow them to follow the path you have for them? Do I trust you to protect them and love them as much as I do? I am sorry that I doubt your love for my children. Remind me daily that your plan for them is so much better than my plan.

My spouse is the love of my life. Forgive me for worrying if you can protect him. You have him in the palm of your hand. He seeks shelter beneath your wings. Please teach me to pray for that protection every day.

El Qanna, please open my eyes and heart. Remove idols from my life. Teach me to trust you more. Teach me to be as generous as you are generous to me. Lord, please forgive me for putting anything in front of you.

Remind me that you are beyond all things. You are more powerful, more loving, all-knowing, and with me every second of every day. Teach me to praise you more daily. Amen.

Questions for Discussion

These questions can be used for personal study or for group discussion.

1. If you could talk to Oprah, what would you tell her about El Qanna?

2. What do you think about your God being jealous?

3. How can El Qanna be both loving and jealous?

4. What tempts you to shift your focus from El Qanna?

5. Where do you see El Qanna in the Old Testament?

6. Where do you see El Qanna in the New Testament?

7. How can you focus more fully on God today? What areas of your life do you need to refocus?

8. What can you do to keep yourself focused on God? List several practical steps you can take to remain focused.

9. How will your increased understanding of God as El Qanna, empower you to fulfill God's mission for you? Write out a prayer to El Qanna claiming the promises and character of God indicated by this Call Sign.

Notes:

6. *ABBA: FATHER*

Abba gives us our mission and comforts us during trials

A godly lady whispered this Call Sign for God after a workshop I taught about His different names a few years ago. I knew it was supposed to be in this book but I really struggled to write about it. Abba means Father. Not just a formal Father but a truly beloved father. It is a term of endearment and focuses on our relationship with God. We are chosen, adopted sons and daughters of Abba. It focuses our minds on God's loving care, provision, and discipline, as well as how to talk to God in prayer.

***
Abba is loving, kind, merciful, and mighty.
***

For me, it brought up memories of my daddy. To this day, I call my earthly father "Daddy" even though he passed away in 1996 from colon cancer when he was only 64. He was the center of my world. As the middle girl of three and as close to a son as my daddy ever had, I grew up a tomboy. I helped my daddy work on cars, repair things, and yell at the Buffalo Bills for playing poorly. I idolized my daddy. He was strong, patient, loving, kind, and passionate. He taught me love and discipline. I knew when he was angry and when he was in a playful mood. Whenever I miss my daddy, I cry out to Abba Father, for comfort, strength and love. He is always willing to hold me while I cry, groan, and throw temper tantrums because I miss my daddy.

I was and still am a strong-willed child. My mom and I would fight quite a bit but I rarely fought with my daddy. When he spoke, I was usually smart enough to listen. I do remember him spanking me because I made my mom cry. He hated seeing her cry but especially if it was because of one of his girls. Because of the discipline, I worked harder on my relationship with my mom. How many times has Abba seen me be mean or short-tempered with His beloved daughters and sons? Abba has never spanked me like my daddy but He has disciplined me to correct me and teach me. Whenever I hurt another person, God will not let me rest until I reconcile with that person. Abba reminds me of His Son's words in Matthew.

> *So if you are offering your gift at the altar and there remember that your brother has something against you, leave your gift there before the altar and go. First, be reconciled to your brother, and then come and offer your gift.*
> Matthew 5:23-24

I need to work to avoid hurting others. Sometimes I speak before I think, other times I am sarcastic, and occasionally I am just mean. God wants me to see all His people as He sees them with eyes of love, forgiveness, and mercy.

***

Abba Father desires us to become more like Him.
***

In many ways, I was the son he never had. My daddy taught me how to change the oil in my car. We worked on his 1952 Bentley Mark VI; he loved restoring "Big Ben." I learned how to drive it and always enjoyed riding beside him. He knew I had a temper and he showed me how to control it. Yet, even now, it is still a battle I fight. Abba also sees my temper and He will send people to allow me to vent so I don't lash out like I really want to. This Call Sign reminds me to keep growing towards Abba. Together we work on my temper and I change slowly but surely.

> *Know this, my beloved brothers: let every person be quick to hear, slow to speak, slow to anger; for the anger of man does not produce the righteousness of God. Therefore put away all filthiness and rampant wickedness and receive with meekness the implanted word, which is able to save your souls.* James 1:12-21

I work on listening, pausing, and thinking before I speak. It takes time and practice but my daddy helped me when I was young, now I rely on my husband to help me. Abba wants me to continue to grow in my faith and my self-control.

I only remember seeing my daddy cry three times. The first was when my older sister was in a very bad car accident. The driver fell asleep, while she was asleep beside him and almost killed her. My daddy was so scared for my sister and mad at the driver that he cried. The second time was at my wedding, which of course, made me cry. The third time was when he met my eldest daughter for the first time. He was such a proud grandpa. I am sure he cried other times, but he was a very private man so he usually avoided crying in public, which is why I remember each time so vividly. He was such a strong man yet he saw crying as a sign of weakness. For His immeasurable strength, Jesus did not avoid crying either. One of the verses people will memorize is John 11:35, "Jesus wept." Jesus experienced all the emotions of being fully human. He went to Abba when He was sad or hurt.

Emotions were created by Abba He understands them and wants to help us learn to handle them correctly. Ephesians 4:32 states, "Be kind to one another, tenderhearted, forgiving one another, as God in Christ forgave you." My daddy forgave the man who almost killed my sister. He showed me what tenderhearted means.

***
Abba enjoys our good times
and holds us tight through our bad times.
***

For a long time, I was angry at God for taking my daddy away. I did not realize how angry at Him I was for many years. It took time working with a counselor to come to terms with my pain in order to embrace the love, forgiveness, grace, and mercy of God. I finally realized God's plan is not my plan. I wanted my daddy to meet all my kids but God's plan allowed me to grow and to rely more on my husband. Once I found healing, my family began to heal and grow together. God's plan for us is a perfect plan, but it may not make sense to us. He will lead us through trials, sadness, good times, and regular days. He is with us and loves us.

My daddy loved storms; loud thunderstorms, heavy snowstorms, and even gentle rain storms. Even now if there is a thunderstorm, I go out on my porch or go to a window to watch it. He taught me how to know how close it was by counting seconds between lightning and thunder. Yet if the storm was very strong, he would have us go inside and sometimes even to the basement to be safe. I remember worrying about him being upstairs when there were tornadoes nearby, while I watched and waited for him to join us in safety. My mother would not let us go near the stairs because if daddy had to come down the stairs, we needed to be far away so he could descend quickly. After snowstorms, he would shovel our driveway clear of every flake of snow then he would help us build sledding runs and frozen forts. Plus, he threw a mean snowball. But he also worried about my reckless nature so he took me to a parking lot during my first winter of driving. He made me do "donuts" (skidding in circles) until I was sick. I have never done a "donut" since. He wanted me to be safe in the snow and not be reckless. Because he knew my nature so well, he knew I would be the one who would try to do "donuts", and crash my car. He worked hard to protect me from myself.

Watching storms roll over the plains in Kansas reminds me of the way Abba displays His power. In 1 Kings 19, we find the prophet Elijah feeling discouraged, attacked, and alone. He cries out to God. God feeds and strengthens him yet Elijah wants more; he wants to see God.

> *And he said, "Go out and stand on the mount before the Lord." And behold, the Lord passed by, and a great and strong wind tore the mountains and broke in pieces the rocks before the Lord, but the Lord was not in the wind. And after the wind an earthquake, but the Lord was not in the earthquake. And after the earthquake a fire, but the Lord was not in the fire. And after the fire the sound of a low whisper. And when Elijah heard it, he wrapped his face in his cloak and went out and stood at the entrance of the cave. And behold, there came a voice to him and said, "What are you doing here, Elijah?"* 1 Kings 19:11-13

God used a storm to show His power, an earthquake, and fire to get Elijah's attention, yet He spoke in a low whisper. Abba can use storms to get our attention, yet He speaks in a low whisper to help us focus on what He is saying. I love to watch storms with my children. I remind them Abba is in control and He wants us to listen to His voice on our missions. He sends us on missions and He will provide us with what we need to accomplish that mission.

I know my daddy was not perfect, he lied to me about smoking which caused his cancer. I do wish I had confronted him about it but I was little and he was my daddy. Abba has never and can never lie, He is Truth. The differences between our worldly fathers and our Heavenly Father all relate to Him being perfectly God and we are imperfect humans who sin.

Sometimes it is our fathers who sin. Some of my friends have fathers who were hurtful, abusive, or absent. All fathers have good traits and bad ones, but no earthly father is capable of protecting their children from all the evil in the world. When they fail us, and they will fail because they are human, we can turn to Abba.

Psalm 89:26 states, "He will cry to Me, 'You are my Father (Abba), My God (Elohim), and the rock of my salvation.'" David cried out to his Abba when he was in need. Abba is our rock. He is our firm foundation. When we have troubles of any kind, we can cry to Him.

***

Abba is the Rock of Our Salvation, our firm foundation.
***

In 1 Samuel 16, God tells Samuel to go meet with Jesse and God will show Samuel who to anoint as the next king. Samuel meets with Jesse. Jesse brings with him his seven sons. In verse 11, Samuel said to Jesse, "Are these all the children? And he (Jesse) said, "There remains yet the youngest, and behold he is tending the sheep. Then Samuel said to Jesse, "Send and bring him; for we will not sit down until he comes here." I hope Jesse did not forget about his youngest son out tending the sheep, but maybe he did. What we do know is God chose David over his older brothers and David never forgot his Heavenly Father.

The first time Abba is used is in Deuteronomy 32.

> *"Do you thus repay the LORD,*
> *you foolish and senseless people?*
> *Is not he, your father [Abba] who created you,*
> *who made you and established you?"*
> Deuteronomy 32:6

This is the start of what we now call the Song of Moses. Moses was about to die and God had chosen Joshua to lead Israel into the Promised Land. God told Moses the people would rebel and they would need a way to remember God's loving-kindness. Moses wrote this song and it is recorded for us in Deuteronomy 32:1-43. Moses proclaimed to the people, Abba has bought them, made them, and established them. Our Abba created us, established us, and through the work of Jesus on the Cross, has redeemed us. We are Abba's adopted sons and daughters. Abba promised He will love us forever. Even Moses knew how much Abba loves us and cares for us; he proclaimed it boldly. Every believer's mission is to share this truth with those they encounter.

Isaiah prophesied about Jesus.

> *"For to us a child is born, to us a son is given, and the government shall be on his shoulder and his name shall be called Wonderful Counselor, Mighty God, Everlasting Father (Abba), Prince of Peace."* Isaiah 9:6

He is our everlasting Father. He never changes, He loves us perfectly. This verse reminds us of the Trinity: God the Father, Jesus, and the Holy Spirit. Even as Jesus was born, this prophecy reminds us of His love, His perfect plan for our salvation.

***

Abba loves us enough to send us the perfect sacrifice.
***

God sent us Jesus to be the perfect sacrifice as well as our High Priest above all high priests. Psalm 110:4 states, "The Lord has sworn and will not change His mind, You are a priest forever after the order of Melchizedek." Abba doesn't change His mind, He will always love us and forgive us. We do not deserve it but His great mercy and grace flow over us each and every day.

> *"I will be to him a father, and he shall be to me a son. I will not take my steadfast love from him, as I took it from him who was before you,"*
> 1 Chronicles 17:13

This verse is about the relationship between Abba and Jesus. Jesus was God's one and only son. In 1 Chronicles 22:10, God says, *"He shall build a house for my name. He shall be my son and I will be his father (Abba), and I will establish his royal throne in Israel forever."* God proclaims Jesus will be king forever. He will come again in glory to defeat Satan.

Jesus spoke to his Abba. In Mark 14:36 Jesus prayed to God: *"And He was saying, "Abba, Father, all things are possible for you. Remove this cup from me. Yet not what I will, but what you will."* Jesus pleaded with Abba to not crucify him. Jesus shared his heart with God. He wanted to obey and share his heart, but he also did not want to keep anything from God. When we hide things from our earthly fathers, they usually find out. I learned it was better to confess than to allow my father to find out on his own. As children of God, we should share all our mistakes with Abba. We should want to let Him have the freedom to come into all areas of our lives.

***

Jesus did not change His mission, but He cried out to Abba.

***

Abba reminds me I have the freedom to choose. Freedom to choose to believe in Him or reject Him. Freedom to choose to obey or rebel. Freedom to choose who I love, like, or reject. When I met and then married my wonderful husband in 1991, I knew it was hard on my daddy to let go of me, even though he liked my choice. He had to let someone else take care of me. He had to trust my husband to treat me well and provide for me.

Just as our earthly fathers allow us to learn from our mistakes, so does our Heavenly Father. I have made many mistakes. My mom and dad showed me no matter how many mistakes I made, they still loved me. They also allowed me to suffer the consequences of my poor choices. That is exactly what Abba does, our choices come with consequences.

When I was little, I did not like the "water rule" my parents made. Their rule was "do not go near the water, because you might fall in." I understood they were trying to protect me but I wanted to see what was in the water. Every time I was near the water, I would fall in and daddy would reach down and save me. The arm he used to save me would get soaking wet and was also the one with his watch. My mom tried buying him "water-resistant" watches, but he would say "they may be water-resistant but they are not Jennifer resistant." When my daddy passed away, my mom gave me all the watches he had kept after I did not obey the "water rule." There were so many ruined watches. My daddy would discipline me after each episode, but I was and still am a strong-willed child. I had to almost drown several times to learn to be careful around water.

Just because my daddy allowed me to learn about the dangers of water does not mean he did not love me. Jesus allows us to experience the world and all its temptations. This does not mean He does not love us. We were created with free will so each one of us can learn things in our own special way. Our choices shape who we are and what we become. God made us each to be our own person with our own unique temptations and trials.

People have asked me about suffering. "If God is Abba, why does He allow us to suffer?" We suffer because of sin in this world and the choices we make. When we become Christians, we make a choice to become part of God's family. We will suffer because the world does not understand God's love or accept His forgiveness. Jesus suffered through the world's rejection so we could have life eternal. Paul states how we are to react to suffering.

> *For all who are led by the Spirit of God are sons of God. For you did not receive the spirit of slavery leading to fall back into fear, but you have received the Spirit of adoption as sons, by who we cry, Abba! Father!" The Spirit himself bears witness with our spirit that we are children of God, and if children, then heirs--heirs of God and fellow heirs with Christ, provided we suffer with him in order that we may be glorified with him.*
> Romans 8:14-17

When I am faced with suffering, I cry out to Abba to help me. Jesus called out to Abba when he was faced with crucifixion.

***

Abba is the Call Sign I call on when my heart is breaking.
***

My heartbreak is usually related to one of my children. I cry out to Abba to help my children because I know His faithfulness. My children need to learn about His faithfulness. They may think they know about God but as they grow, they will learn more and more. I love the verse in Isaiah about Abba.

> *But now, O LORD, you are our Father (Abba),*
> *we are the clay, and you are our potter;*
> *we are all the work of your hand.*

Isaiah 64:8

We are the clay which needs to be kneaded and shaped. Abba kneads us and softens us so He can make us into what He needs us to be. When we allow Him to shape us, we can be used to serve Him through the missions He calls us to accomplish. When I buy new pottery, I don't just buy all of the same types of pieces. If all I had was a plate, I would make a huge mess trying to eat soup. If all I had was a bowl, cutting a steak would be very hard. The Potter kneads, bends, and shapes us into the form we need to be to be able to complete His mission for us.

Abba makes each of us into the person He desires us to become, a person who is more loving, more caring, more like Him. As it says in Ephesians:

> *And he gave the apostles, the prophets, the evangelists, the shepherds, and teachers, to equip the saints for the works of ministry, for building up of the body of Christ, until we all attain to the unity of the faith, and of the knowledge of the Son of God, to mature manhood, to the measure of the stature of the fullness of Christ.* Ephesians 4:11-13

Each of us has a job to do for our Abba. We need to focus on our job as we follow His will. When I focus on others' missions or envy their positions, my job may appear less needed or valuable. Yet, my Abba calls me to do what He designed me to do. He calls you, too. Paul repeats this idea in his letter to the church at Corinth.

> *If one member suffers, all suffer together; if one member is honored, all rejoice together. Now you are the body of Christ and individually members of it. And God has appointed in the church, first apostles, second prophets, third teachers, then miracles, then gifts of healings, helping, administrating, various kinds of tongues. Are all apostles? Are all prophets? Are all teachers? Do all work miracles? Do all possess gifts of healing? Do all speak with tongues? Do all interpret?* 1 Corinthians 12:26-30

***

Satan's attacks on any part of the body of believers, affect the whole body.

***

Praying for those suffering and helping them is part of what Abba wants us to do. The church is supposed to help each other in times of trial and trouble, as well as rejoice together when things go well. Many times, it seems if one church is growing other groups try to stop its growth. Instead, we are supposed to rejoice with them. We are supposed to be different from the world and work together to share the Gospel.

Abba wants His family to have unity. My daddy hated it when my sisters and I fought. He would escape to his basement workshop to avoid our bickering and our hormones. Our Heavenly Father does not avoid us. He wants us to have unity and love. He is active all the time to grow us and mold us into the vessel He wants us to be.

> *"And if you call on him as Father (Abba) who judges impartially according to each one's deeds, conduct yourselves with fear throughout the time of your exile, knowing that you were ransomed from the futile ways inherited from your forefathers, not with perishable things such as silver or gold, but with the precious blood of Christ, like that of a lamb without blemish or spot."* 1 Peter 1:17-19

Notice in these verses Abba and judge are together. Just because He is our Abba, our Father, does not mean He won't judge. He must judge, for He cannot have sin in His presence. But keep reading. He redeemed us by the precious blood of Christ. He wants us to be in heaven with Him. He wants us to look at Him with love in our eyes. He is our perfect Father. Our Heavenly Father won't let us down; He loves us and He wants us to become more like Himself.

This is not the last Call Sign, but in many ways, it is one of the most important. It reminds us He wants a deep relationship with us. He wants us to tell Him everything and share our hearts, minds and lives with him.

> *For you are our Father,*
> *though Abraham does not know us,*
> *and Israel does not acknowledge us;*
> *you, O LORD, are our Father,*

our Redeemer from old is your name.
Isaiah 63:16

Our earthly fathers are not perfect but Abba is perfect, unchanging, loving, and merciful. His love is perfect and never-ending. Although this Call Sign challenges me, it also reminds me of His love. He loves me when I disobey and stomp my feet, follow my plan and not His, yell at Him, and even when I need Him to hold me when my spirit is crushed. Abba takes all I have and cares for me no matter what. He is love.

When you need strength, help, comfort, or wisdom, you can cry out to Abba Father to give you what you need when you need it to keep walking in line with the mission He has for you.

Prayer to Abba

Abba, Father we love you. You surround us with your loving arms. You pull us in and hold us tight. Thank you for caring for every tear that falls. Thank you for loving us even when we feel unlovable.

When our days are full of activities, You cheer us on. When we are too busy, You whisper, "Slow down." You send us rainbows and gentle breezes to remind us to pause and slow down. When we are with our families You teach us to laugh and enjoy time together.

There are days when life is tough, You are there. You are in the midst of the pain of losing a loved one. You hold us when our children or our parents are hurting. You stand beside us during memorial services and by gravestones. You are with us.

When life hands us lemons, You remind us to make lemonade. When the military sends us to a place we do not want to go, You go before us and prepare a place for us. When we are leaving behind friends and family, You show us new people to embrace as friends, and some become family. You do not leave us alone. Abba, Father you are with us.

Sometimes we wander far from Your will. You correct us. We may get mad and stomp our feet like a two-year-old but You are patient and long-suffering. You want us to choose the best path, not the easiest path. You walk through hard and easy places with us. You may discipline us but that is because You love us.

You are love. Abba, Father, teach us to love others as You love us. Teach us to become more like you every day. Abba Father as we cry out in pain, let us feel your loving arms around us.

Amen.

Questions for Discussion

These questions can be used for personal study or for group discussion.

1. Where do you see Abba in the Old Testament?

2. Where do you find Abba in the New Testament?

3. 1 Peter 1:17-19 puts Abba with the Judge. Why do you think Peter calls God both Abba and Judge? How does that change your view of Abba?

4. What traits are important to you in a father. What makes a person a "daddy" as opposed to being a "father"?

5. What do you learn about Abba from the following verses? Memorize your favorite verse from the list.

   a. Galatians 4:6

   b. Romans 8:15

   c. 1 John 3:1

   d. James 1:17

6. How will your increased understanding of God as Abba, empower you to fulfill God's mission for you? Write out a prayer to Abba claiming the promises and character of God indicated by this Call Sign.

Notes:

Charlie Mike: Continue The Mission

For me, learning about The Call Signs of God is an ongoing mission. He gave me this mission over ten years ago and I am still moving forward. Along the way, He also gave me some short-term missions and a few longer missions. Every mission from God is part of His Great Commission.

> *And Jesus came and said to them, "All authority in heaven and on earth has been given to me. Go therefore and make disciples of all nations, baptizing them in the name of the Father and of the Son and of the Holy Spirit, teaching them to observe all that I have commanded you.*
> *And behold, I am with you always, to the end of the age."*
> Matthew 28:18-20

Each mission in the military has many parts. Wherever there are "boots on the ground" there will be service members supporting them with fuel, food, intelligence, and vehicles. These missions rarely just use one branch of the service. Teams crossover to help each other. The Air Force can "Bring the Rain", the Navy can move massive amounts of weapons and people around the world. Just as a single military mission can take hundreds of people working together, Jehovah wants us to work together to share His love. His mission for you will be different from mine because you have different abilities, gifts, and desires.

As Elohim, He gave me the mission of raising three kids to love and serve Him. There were days I did not think I would make it but Elohim saw my struggles and encouraged me. When I had nothing left to give El Shaddai breathed His life-giving power into me. This decades-long mission is not complete and will continue until He calls me home.

El Elyon, the Lord Most High, has taught me to fast and pray. Prayer is a daily need for all of us. Asking to join Abba each day with what He wants us to do makes the days easier to bear. Not all days will be easy and many times our circumstances will be beyond our ability to influence, but even in trials, our Adonai is in control. Trials and trails can lead us closer to God when we call on Him using His Call Signs, trusting we can rest under His wings and His protection.

He knows our missions and our heart's desires. El Qanna will pursue us through the Holy Spirit and give us strength. Even though we are called to fear God, this idea is not popular and many churches do not talk about it. People do not want to fear God. They want to only think of Him as Abba, Father. This view misses the truth about God. He is above and beyond anything we can understand. His power and might are amazing. Because He is perfect He cannot be with things that are not perfect. God wants us to learn *all* about Him and the totality of His character.

His Call Signs are characteristics, but He is so much more. He is the Alpha and Omega, the Beginning and the End. He wants us to learn more about Him, His attributes, His whole Trinity. Focusing on just one part of God means we do not know much about Him. We need to continue to learn about Him to become more like Him. As this book draws to a close, I want you to know the six names of God we studied together are not His only Call Signs. He is so much more. He has called me to continue to learn about other facets of His character. In the Old Testament, He is called Jehovah-Jireh, The Lord Our Provider, or Jehovah-Nissi, The Lord is Our Banner. The more I study, the more His Spirit reveals to me. This is a life-long process and our knowledge won't be complete until we meet Him face to face. But if we ask, He is faithful to provide us with a hunger to know Him more and make Him known in all the places He sends us and all the missions He gives us.

How is God calling you to make Him known today? As you read the Scriptures, watch for other Call Signs, write them down and learn about them. In the Appendix, you will find an example page to help you get started with your study of God's other Call Signs. As we look to God, He wants to show us more about His character and especially His love for us. Don't hesitate to follow Adonai and rely on El Shaddai for strength. I am praying for you to seek out your mission and to boldly seek God every single day.

Jennifer

Sample Call Sign Worksheet

"Then she (Hagar) called the name of the LORD who spoke to her, 'You are a God who sees'; for she said, 'Have I even remained alive here after seeing Him?'"
Genesis 16:13 El Roi

1. Look up Hebrew, Greek, or Aramaic words translated to God using Strong's Concordance. Study the synonyms for the words you find there.

2. Who first used this Call Sign for God?

3. What were the circumstances surrounding this name?

4. Look up other Scriptures where the same words were used.

5. How are the people in those situations similar to or different from you? What did they need from God in their situation? How did He meet that need?

6. What needs might arise as you carry out your God-given mission that would make you call out to God using this particular Call Sign?

7. Who in your life needs to know the character of God as revealed by this Call Sign?

LEADER'S GUIDE

The following pages are designed to support and encourage this study's small group leaders or facilitators. This appendix includes what to do before your group meets the first time, a sample timeline for discussion, general information about the format of the study, and some warnings and help for sections of the study that might touch tender places for participants.

What to Do Before Your First Meeting

1. Pray for Elohim to give you His wisdom and discernment as you lead women through the study.
2. Ask someone to pray for you during your time as a group leader, two to three people would be great.
3. Be sure you have good contact information for each of your participants.
4. Contact them before the first group meeting and see if they have any questions.
5. Dedicate a notebook to use as a group prayer journal during your time together or use note cards which can be collected.
6. Either provide or suggest the ladies purchase a journal or notebook to record what El Elyon teaches them throughout the study. Plus, you can add other Call Signs as you find them.

General Information

Each meeting of this six-week includes a lesson to help participants focus on one Call Sign of God at a time. Throughout the lesson, I have included some questions to process key concepts. Each week has homework and a sample prayer. The questions serve as your material for discussion during class. Keep in mind that you may not have time to cover them all. As you pray for your class and your lesson each week, highlight or mark the questions the Holy Spirit prompts you to be sure to discuss. Ask your participants if they had a question they particularly wanted to discuss or one they didn't understand.

As a facilitator, it isn't your job to know all the answers. It's El Shaddai's job. It is okay to say you don't know and then seek a study resource, chaplain, or pastor to help you learn the answer before the next meeting.

Consider some of the following for your first group meeting.
- Be sure to discuss the best way to communicate with each participant as they sign up for the group.
- Pass around the journal or notecards at the beginning of class and ask ladies to write down their requests or praises.
- Begin and end each class on time.
- Don't be afraid of silence. Give participants time to chime in before you tell them all the answers. Pay attention to who does most of the talking and invite those who are quieter to share their insights as well.

Sample Timeline

0900 – Open with prayer.

> Pass around the prayer journal or hand out the note cards.

0905 – Welcome the ladies to the Bible study.

> At the beginning of the first meeting, share 2-3 things you would like the ladies to know about yourself. Allow the ladies to share their name and one thing about themselves.

0915 – Give a brief summary of the week's lesson.

0920 – Share what impacted you most during the week's lesson. Hit the highlights that spoke to your heart.

0925 – Ask the ladies to share what impacted them.

0935 – Use chapter questions to guide the discussion. Prioritize questions you'd like to cover as you work through each week's lesson. You know your group, so feel free to pick and choose the questions that would be most relevant.

0955 – Close your Bible study time in prayer. If you're comfortable and it is appropriate to the group dynamics, include the requests ladies wrote in the journal or on notecards.

APPENDIX A:
How to Read the Bible for Personal Study

Your Word is a lamp to my feet and a light to my path. Psalm 119:105

Studying the Bible for personal use is life changing! We are transformed by what we learn when we read God's word. We can study the Bible in a group or alone. We study the Bible to get answers, gain guidance, avoid wrong teaching, and to learn about Abba. Yet, our approach to the Bible matters:

- **Approach the Bible prayerfully.** Ask the Holy Spirit to use God's Word to transform you.

- **Approach the Bible expectantly.** Expect to encounter El Qanna in His living word.

- **Approach the Bible carefully.** Read verses in context, asking who, what, when, and why.

- **Approach the Bible thoughtfully.** Record your thoughts and reflections.

When to Read the Bible: You can read the Bible anytime! I like to read the Bible first thing in the morning to frame my day, yet as a mom sometimes life starts earlier than I expect. You don't have to read the Bible just once a day either. Anytime you have a few moments for reflection and meditation, the Bible is great inspiration—especially Psalms and Proverbs.

Study Aids: Many Bibles have comments and explanations. Read the Scripture first before turning to the notes. This method allows you to discern the Truth firsthand. A good study Bible gives some background on each book and tells who wrote it, when and why. If you have questions or concerns, find a solid Bible teacher, or chaplain to help you. The Lord has gifted teachers who correctly understand and obey the truth. A good teacher helps us learn the right way to keep in step with Adonai.

Bottom Line: Approach the Bible prayerfully and humbly for a deeper understanding. Study verses in context and seek explanations from mature, seasoned Christians.

APPENDIX B:
How to Memorize Scripture

For whatever was written in former days was written for our instruction, that through endurance and through the encouragement of the Scriptures we might have hope.
Romans 15:4

Elohim's word is foundational to our spiritual maturity. Storing God's word in our heart means we have the truth whenever and wherever we need it. We do this by memorizing key and essential verses. Memorization allows Scripture to "take root."

Memorizing information, especially Holy Scripture, is essential. Smartphones break, iPads lose energy, and we can't carry our computer on our back. We must remember important information. A pilot can't always fly on autopilot, nor can a captain trust he knows where his ship is in the ocean. I understand it's not easy. Our memory muscles need development. But the more we use our memory muscle, the stronger it gets.

Tips for Memorizing Scripture:

- Find a quiet place, free from distractions.

- Read the verse(s) at least 3X: first for the eyes, second for the mind, third for the heart.

- Say the verse out loud—speak it with understanding.

- Write it down. Carry it with you and refer to it during down times (in line to check out, before a meeting starts, etc.).

- Read the passage at night before lights out. You will be amazed what your mind does while you are sleeping! You may awake with the words on your tongue!

Memorization can be a little frustrating at first. But the rewards are remarkable. Take your time.

Memorizing helps us capture each word and remember it in the future. Being involved with the verse makes memorization easier. Other methods of memorization, such as using music, might help you. Repetition is important.

The goal is to let El Elyon's Word get deep into the recesses of your heart. Having a memorized verse spring up at just the right moment is encouraging and life-changing!

APPENDIX C:
How to Pray

Do not be anxious about anything but in everything by prayer and supplication with thanksgiving let your requests be made known to God.
Philippians 4:6

When we pray, we reach out to God. In the reaching, our attitude and spiritual awareness are changed. Prayer is not some magical formula to get the right results. God is not a magician, it is not one of His Call Signs. Prayer is a relationship. Abba desires real and personal communication with us. He's more interested in what concerns us than how we pray. Prayer is personal.

In Matthew 6:9-13 Jesus taught his disciples to pray. Many people use this as a pattern for prayer, and others use it as a daily prayer. Some do both!

Pray then like this: "Our Father in heaven, hallowed be your name. Your kingdom come, your will be done, on earth as it is in heaven. Give us this day our daily bread, and forgive us our debts, as we also have forgiven our debtors. And lead us not into temptation, but deliver us from evil.
Matthew 6:9-13

The book of Psalms is full of beautiful prayers. We can pray these back to Adonai, or we can speak to Him and praise Him freely and personally. Though we can (and should) pray anywhere, Jesus often took extended periods of time and went to solitary places to pray. What should we pray about? Anything and everything! When you pray, remember this: Prayer is personal!

Draw near to God and He will draw near to you.
James 4:8

- **Pray about everything.** There are no secrets with the all-knowing God.
- **Pray with confidence.** El Qanna is not judging the delivery of your prayers!
- **Pray with thankfulness.** Gratitude is one of the ways El Elyon guards our hearts.

APPENDIX D
What Does It Mean to Be a Christian?

"Whoever believes and is baptized will be saved"

Mark 16:16a

What does it mean to be a Christian? It means believing in the Lord Jesus for salvation. Believing Christ is God is an intellectual belief. Giving Him Lordship of your life implies following His leadership—learning His ways and walking in them.

A Christian is a Christ-follower, a student, or a disciple. Being a Christian is much like being a military service member because it requires faith, commitment, and trust. Being a Christian means bearing Christ's name and surrendering to His leadership, sometimes at great personal cost. Our choices during our lifetime are to only for a short time, but our commitment to Christ lasts for eternity.

If the idea of being a Christian is new to you, consider the following truths:

> *Jesus said to him, "I am the way, and the truth, and the life. No one comes to the Father except through me."* John 14:6

> *For God so loved the world, that he gave his only Son, that whoever believes in him should not perish but have eternal life.* John 3:16

> *For Christ also suffered once for sins, the righteous for the unrighteous, that he might bring us to God, being put to death in the flesh but made alive in the spirit.* 1 Peter 3:18

> *If we confess our sins, he is faithful and just to forgive us our sins and to cleanse us from all unrighteousness.* 1 John 1:9

It simply takes a sincere prayer to be saved. If you need a little help, use the following prayer.

> *Lord Jesus, I have sinned against you. I come to you today with an open and seeking heart asking you to forgive my sins. I believe You are the Son*

of God. You came to earth and chose to die on the cross for my sins, and then rose again so I could have eternal life. Beginning today, I give You my heart, my soul, my life to you. In the wonderful name of Jesus. Amen.

If you prayed this prayer, please speak to your Bible study leader, a Christian friend, or a pastor. They can help you continue to learn more and grow in your walk with God.

Endnotes:

CHAPTER 1
1. Elwell, W. A., & Beitzel, B. J. (1988). Elohim. In Baker encyclopedia of the Bible (Vol. 1, p. 697). Grand Rapids, MI: Baker Book House.

2. pg 97 "The Five Love Languages: How to Express Heartfelt Commitment to Your Mate." by Gary Chapman Northfield Publishing Chicago ILL cc 2004

CHAPTER 3
1. Definition from http://thebondservant.org/?page_id=68

CHAPTER 5
1. http://blogs.blackvoices.com/2008/07/02/oprah-denies-jesus-as-sole-way-to-god

2. http://Raa.prlog.org/10059098-is-god-jealous-of-oprah-how-does-oprah-reconcile-spirituality-religion-the-biggest-question.html

3. https://www.merriam-webster.com/dictionary/tolerance

4. MacMillan, John Mark. "How He Loves" Church Music. Sixsteps/Sparrow Records, 2009

More Books by Jennifer Wake

He Is Jehovah: How Knowing the Names of God Encourages Women to Share His Faithfulness can be purchased at:

https://www.amazon.com/He-Jehovah-Knowing-Encourages-Faithfulness

Let's Connect

You can find me at https://www.jenniferwake.com

Facebook: https://www.facebook.com/mom23wakes
Instagram: https://www.instagram.com/mom23wakes/
Pinterest: https://www.pinterest.com/mom23wakes/
Twitter: https://twitter.com/mom23wakes

www.ingramcontent.com/pod-product-compliance
Lightning Source LLC
Chambersburg PA
CBHW082246090526
44585CB00021BA/2465